30 Ten-Minute Plays for 3 Actors
from Actors Theatre of Louisville's
National Ten-Minute Play Contest

SMITH AND KRAUS PUBLISHERS
Contemporary Playwrights / Collections

Act One Festival '95

EST Marathon '94: The One-Act Plays
EST Marathon '95: The One-Act Plays
EST Marathon '96: The One-Act Plays
EST Marathon '97: The One-Act Plays
EST Marathon '98: The One-Act Plays

Humana Festival: 20 One-Act Plays 1976–1996
Humana Festival '93: The Complete Plays
Humana Festival '94: The Complete Plays
Humana Festival '95: The Complete Plays
Humana Festival '96: The Complete Plays
Humana Festival '97: The Complete Plays
Humana Festival '98: The Complete Plays
Humana Festival '99: The Complete Plays
Humana Festival 2000: The Complete Plays

Women Playwrights: The Best Plays of 1992
Women Playwrights: The Best Plays of 1993
Women Playwrights: The Best Plays of 1994
Women Playwrights: The Best Plays of 1995
Women Playwrights: The Best Plays of 1996
Women Playwrights: The Best Plays of 1997
Women Playwrights: The Best Plays of 1998
Women Playwrights: The Best Plays of 1999

If you require prepublication information about upcoming Smith and Kraus books, you may receive our semi-annual catalogue, free of charge, by sending your name and address to *Smith and Kraus Catalogue, 4 Lower Mill Road, North Stratford, NH 03590. Or call us at (800) 895-4331, fax (603) 643-1831. www.SmithKraus.com.*

30 Ten-Minute Plays for 3 Actors
from Actors Theatre of Louisville's National Ten-Minute Play Contest

Edited by Michael Bigelow Dixon, Amy Wegener, and Stephen Moulds

Contemporary Playwrights Series

SK
A Smith and Kraus Book

A Smith and Kraus Book
Published by Smith and Kraus, Inc.
177 Lyme Road, Hanover, NH 03755
www.SmithKraus.com

Manufactured in the United States of America

Cover and Text Design by Julia Hill Gignoux, Freedom Hill Design
Layout by Jennifer McMaster
Cover Photography by Richard Trigg
Cover Photo: *Arabian Nights* by David Ives
(l-r: Gretchen Lee Krich, Ellen Lauren and Will Bond)

First Edition: September 2001
10 9 8 7 6 5 4 3 2 1

Library of Congress Cataloguing-in-Publication Data
Contemporary Playwrights Series
30 ten-minute plays for 3 actors from Actors Theatre of Louisville's National Ten-Minute Play Contest / edited by Michael Bigelow Dixon, Amy Wegener, and Stephen Moulds. —1st ed.
p. c.m — (Contemporary playwrights series)
ISBN 1-57525-278-3
1. One-act plays, American. I. Title: Thirty ten-minute plays for three actors from Actors Theatre of Louisville's National Ten-Minute Play Contest. II.Dixon, Michael Bigelow.
III. Wegener, Amy. IV. Moulds, Stephen. V. Actors Theatre of Louisville. VI. Series.

PS627.O53 A17 2001
812'.04108054—dc21
2001034484

Contents

Acknowledgments

Thanks to the following persons for their invaluable assistance in compiling
this volume of plays:

Brendan Healy

Rosalind Heinz

Robert D. Kemnitz

Jennifer McMaster

Tanya Palmer

Karen Petruska

Jeffrey Rodgers

Alexander Speer

Richard Trigg

Introduction

Like the engine of a Formula One race car, all the moving parts of the ten-minute play—the revelation of character, the development of conflict, the investigation of theme—need to be precision-tuned for the play to get from start to finish in only ten minutes and still have a meaningful impact. One remarkable thing about this collection of short plays is that each of the playwrights fine-tunes her or his work in a unique way. The individuality of each script suggests there may be countless ways to run the ten-minute gauntlet, which is good news for playwrights who might otherwise feel constrained by a time limitation. Furthermore, the impressive variety of subject matter and style in this collection promises something for everyone.

ACTORS: One virtue of the ten-minute form is that dramatic action is derived from character illumination, interaction, and change. There's not much time for anything else. Just like any other play, the roles require a detailed formulation of character back story, the consideration of complex motivations, and continual reaction and adjustment to changing tactics and objectives inside relationships. There's as much time in the play as you need to do this work, but not much to spare.

DIRECTORS AND DESIGNERS: These ten-minute plays are complete, self-contained dramatic works, replete with imagery, metaphor, action, theme, and structure. They permit the same work in analysis and interpretation as much longer plays while emphasizing selectivity, conciseness, and focus. In the ten-minute play every detail counts, and although that's true of longer plays as well, the brevity of the modern rehearsal period still provides sufficient time to pay attention to all the details of a ten-minute play in production.

PLAYWRIGHTS: How is it possible to get it all done in ten minutes? Investigate character, orchestrate conflict, develop relationship, examine ideas, and finish it all with an insight or two into the human condition? Well, here are thirty examples to study. These playwrights begin with the eternal triangle in human relationships and then explore the inevitable competition and jealousy, division,s and disagreements. On stage, two may be company, but two against one is a fascinating crowd.

DRAMATURGS: What does it mean, the amazing popularity of the ten-minute play? Does it speak to the shortness of attention spans in these sound-bitten times? Or does it bespeak the exhaustion of narrative imagination as a result of overexposure to the media? Actually, we think the popularity of the form relates most significantly to the need for and rewards of diverse expression at the turn of the twenty-first century. Because you can produce five of these plays in an hour or eight in two hours with an intermission, an evening of ten-minute plays offers a range of aesthetic ideas and cultural viewpoints for both audiences and artists. Also, more writers get heard in one evening of ten-minute plays than get produced in a month at most professional theaters—and for those of us who are interested in developing new voices for the stage, that's not an insignificant fact.

TEACHERS: Written by American playwrights at the turn of the twenty-first century, these plays tend to address topics which today's students can relate to: sex, religion, violence, self-image, success, gender roles, politics, and art. Most of these plays hold a mirror up to young people's lives, and that gives any teacher a huge advantage in the classroom, whether they're teaching literature, creative writing, or acting.

PRODUCERS: Looking for a way to involve more actors, directors, designers, and playwrights at your theater? Hoping to expand or experiment with your company's repertoire? Dreaming of attracting more diverse and younger audiences? Consider producing a bill of ten-minute plays. An evening of these works offers many of the same rewards as a musical revue: energy, variety, and the fail-safe factor of brevity, which guarantees that even the least successful work will be finished in ten minutes.

Finally, these thirty plays are part of an anthologized trilogy featuring ninety plays. These plays have been selected from the 25,000 ten-minute plays submitted by playwrights since 1990 to the annual National Ten-Minute Play Contest at Actors Theatre of Louisville. So here are the stand-outs, written by the already famous, soon-to-be famous, and should-be famous playwrights who've helped energize the past decade of American theater with their creative contributions in the ten-minute form.

— *Michael Bigelow Dixon, Amy Wegener, and Stephen Moulds*

Plays
for
Three Men

Singleton, the Medal Winner
by Thomas Babe

CHARACTERS

CHUBBS: The surgeon, twenties.

SINGLETON: The soldier, twenties.

DAVIS, MAN'S VOICE: Both twenties (same actor).

TIME

1863.

Singleton, the Medal Winner

Scene 1

A Civil War–vintage Union flag upstage. Downstage, Singleton, the wounded soldier, suspended on a plank tilted toward us from giant scales. The arrow on the face of the scales reads 144 pounds. Nearby, in a bloody coat and holding a brown bottle and spoon, is the surgeon, Chubbs.

SINGLETON: Can you save me?

CHUBBS: I can do my best. But not how you were. Not in one piece. The leg will have to go. It is your *vulni lutulici.* Also…I fear you have contracted erysipelas. Take it how you will—you've lost nearly all the meat on your body.

(Steamboat whistle sounds quite near.)

SINGLETON: Can you make my pain, though, stand its distance? *(Chubbs gets up, pours brown liquid into the spoon, and ladles it down Singleton's throat. Singleton smacks his lips.)* That's whiskey—all that is.

CHUBBS: That's all I know that works anymore.

(Steamboat whistle again.)

SINGLETON: We're taking on ice.

CHUBBS: That's right. That's very good.

SINGLETON: The blocks'll be sliding down right under us. *(Imitating the sounds.)* Shirrr-skissss-bonk! Shirrr-skiss-bonk! Last time, or time before last, Nurse McInerney was saying, one block cut loose and smashed open three coffins. *(Pause.)* When I'm to be buried on the shore, leave a barrel stave stuck in the mud with my name on it. In ink. So the boys can find me and take me home.

CHUBBS: They won't want you like that—thin and in the ground for weeks.

SINGLETON: They won't care.

CHUBBS: You're going to make it.

SINGLETON: No.

CHUBBS: You're going to make it.

SINGLETON: No. You have me on the weighing machine.

CHUBBS: You don't know why I have you on the weighing machine.

SINGLETON: To measure when my soul flees.

CHUBBS: I am a surgeon. You can't know half what I know. Don't make me despise you.

(Captain Davis, in a well-traveled uniform, comes in.)

CHUBBS: Yes?

DAVIS: I am here to arrange presentation to... *(Looks at his papers.)* ...Joseph Singleton—of his medal.

SINGLETON: For what?

DAVIS: I don't know. Don't you know?

SINGLETON: No.

DAVIS: *(To Chubbs.)* Can I do this in about one hour?

CHUBBS: Give him the medal now.

DAVIS: I don't have it. They're taking it on. With the other supplies.

SINGLETON: And the ice. Shirrr-skisss-bonk. Where does the ice come from? Do you know where the ice comes from? In this heat, where do they find it?

DAVIS: I don't know.

CHUBBS: It's stored up to the North.

(Sound of the ice beneath. Shirrr-skisss-bonk. Shirrr-skisss-bonk.)

SINGLETON: Can you get me a sliver of ice, please, to wet my lips with?

(Chubbs and Davis look at each other. Blackout.)

Scene 2

Singleton sits by himself, his rifle upright under his arm. He has one boot off and is thoughtfully picking at his toes.

SINGLETON: *(Calling softly.)* Where you at?

MAN'S VOICE: Where I was.

SINGLETON: Should I come over?

MAN'S VOICE: Can you reach me?

SINGLETON: I can do my best. What's here between us?

MAN'S VOICE: Where they shoot so well.

SINGLETON: Sharper's Alley. Would you be the one, then, doing all the bush-whacking?

MAN'S VOICE: I'm hungry.

SINGLETON: I'll be right over. I've got cartridges here and some biscuits and bacon. I put a gun to the quartermaster's son-of-a-bitching head. All the men are hungry, I told him. All the men are sick and tired and hungry.

MAN'S VOICE: I'm thirsty.

SINGLETON: That's okay, too. I got a block of ice.

(Very distant steamboat whistle.)

MAN'S VOICE: Where's ice come from this time of year?

SINGLETON: From a polar bear's mansion to the North. *(Pause.)* You have a fever?

MAN'S VOICE: Like lightning in my chest.

SINGLETON: I have lice. And I cut myself in the hand paring an apple at Gettysburg. My *vulni lutulici. (Pause.)* And I have something wrong in the middle of me. Below the middle of me. It's hard and sore.

MAN'S VOICE: Leave off talking about it.

(Singleton puts on his boot and stands up.)

SINGLETON: Hard and sore and hot...and, I don't recall what else. Well, I'm coming over.

MAN'S VOICE: You want to die?

SINGLETON: I just want to be over there—with you.

MAN'S VOICE: You don't really have no food.

SINGLETON: Some.

MAN'S VOICE: No cartridges.

SINGLETON: Some.

MAN'S VOICE: No cake of ice.

SINGLETON: No. But I thought of a cake of ice.

MAN'S VOICE: You *do* want to die.

SINGLETON: No, I don't want to die. I want to nearly die. But first, I want to be over there with you. So you will remember me. Forever. Till you are extinguished by some shot or shell. My name is Joseph Singleton.

MAN'S VOICE: Joseph Singleton. Your face sounds like another face I heard just recently.

SINGLETON: You've never pictured my face.

MAN'S VOICE: In a polar bear's mansion. *(Laughs harshly.)*

SINGLETON: I'm having trouble with you. Tell me, then. Are you fair? Or are you dark? Short? Tall? Disfigured somewise? Do you sport calluses on your hands?

MAN'S VOICE: I was a blacksmith once. I sport calluses on my hands.

SINGLETON: Good. Now—how much do you weigh?

MAN'S VOICE: Less.

SINGLETON: I weigh more. I used to be a feather. But lately, I've been feasting on bits of the men I've killed.

MAN'S VOICE: You never killed nobody.

SINGLETON: I thought about it though. That made me fat.

MAN'S VOICE: I despise you.

SINGLETON: Ah, but... Didn't we love each other once? Wasn't that the purpose? Didn't I court you under your window—and you threw me down the toy soldier you had guarding Mister Lincoln in his white mansion made of ice.

MAN'S VOICE: I threw you down a horse ball.

SINGLETON: Well, I caught it, then, and saved it—as I did our first kiss.

MAN'S VOICE: I didn't know you ever.

(Distant steamboat whistle.)

SINGLETON: We begun in the glory days, when I carried the flag and I never wavered for an instant because I was good—and my heart was high and true. I did it all for you, and now you despise me. But some good will come of it still. Of all this death and pig-smell. All this endless pig-smell I find all over myself. So... *(Pause.)* If I crawl across on my belly, I won't be but rump-shot. If I slip up and put my leg in the air, they'll take that. But, if perchance my head should rise—it'd blow up like a cantaloupe. All them many risks I'd take just to see the sweet face of my enemy.

MAN'S VOICE: Go shit and fall in it.

(Distant steamboat whistle.)

SINGLETON: *(Taking the first step.)* They might even give me a medal, you know.

MAN'S VOICE: DON'T COME HERE!

SINGLETON: *(Taking another step.)* But I bring you a sliver of ice—for your fevered lips.

MAN'S VOICE: DON'T COME HERE, I SAY!

(Gunshot nearby. Then the distant steamboat whistle.)

SINGLETON: Hello? *(Pause.)* Hello? *(Pause.)* Son of a bitch! He shot himself!

(Singleton cocks his rifle and points it directly into his own leg. He squints his eyes shut. As he is pulling the trigger... Blackout—and in the blackout, a gunshot.)

Scene 3

The flag, the plank bed and scales. Singleton, asleep. Chubbs sits, holding his hand.

CHUBBS: I do despise you, you know—you and your sort. The rest of them applaud you. Your courage and manhood as depicted in the newspapers. And in many a vacant bed from here to Utica, the lonely maidens rub their underbellies and moan. They're thinking of you, soldier, not of me. No one ever thinks of me.

(Singleton suddenly squeezes Chubbs's hand very hard and opens his eyes.)

SINGLETON: You mustn't be bitter.

CHUBBS: I'm sorry. There are so many of you—and so little I know how to do.

SINGLETON: Make your heart cold, then.

CHUBBS: I do the best I can. *(Pause.)* Whiskey?

SINGLETON: Yes, thank you. *(Chubbs doses Singleton.)* I know you do the best you can. I know that in my heart.

CHUBBS: Thank you. *(Pause.)* Tell me about the war, then, about your brave adventures—the adventures you, yourself, may not have seen as brave.

SINGLETON: Oh, it wasn't much. I was a toy soldier. I played in the scorching heat as I used to romp with my friends in the snow. Some of them died. I wanted some of them to die—so I could live longer. *(Looking up.)* How much do I weigh now?

CHUBBS: About the same.

SINGLETON: How much will I weigh after?

CHUBBS: I don't know. A little less, perhaps.

SINGLETON: Doctor, you are pining.

CHUBBS: I am not pining.

SINGLETON: Oh, but you are. Tell me, what are you pining for?

CHUBBS: Whole men. Winter. A ripe juicy peach. The humdrum. What are you pining for, soldier?

SINGLETON: Nothing. I've had all I could stand of every last thing I could ever want. *(Pause.)* One other item—that bit of ice I asked for?

CHUBBS: I had it here. You fell asleep. It melted. I can get you another.

SINGLETON: You needn't worry.

(Singleton closes his eyes again. Chubbs drops his head into his hands. Captain Davis comes in, with a grand little velvet box.)

DAVIS: I have his medal now—and the citation. For unaccountable bravery in attacking and subduing a concentration of hostile sharpshooters. Wake him up. We'll get it done.

CHUBBS: He just passed.

DAVIS: Oh…

(Chubbs wipes his eyes and gets up. He looks at the scales and makes a note on his chart.)

CHUBBS: His soul weighed about the same as the rest.

DAVIS: Does that surprise you?

CHUBBS: I thought it would weigh more.

DAVIS: When you put him in ice, put the medal in there with him, would you?

(Davis hands the box to Chubbs. Then he salutes the corpse of Singleton. And exits. Chubbs opens the box and takes out the medal. He puts the medal—on its brilliant purple ribbon—around his own neck. Then he kisses Singleton on the forehead and sits down. He takes Singleton's hand. Blackout.)

END OF PLAY

Tango Delta
by Jeffrey Hatcher

CHARACTERS

AGENT ONE: Mid-thirties, ustache, well-built.

AGENT TWO: Twenties, trim, clean-shaven.

AGENT THREE: Twenties, shorter, solid.

Various voices heard over walkie-talkies.

SETTING

A rooftop of a tall building overlooking the business district of a large, unnamed city.

Afternoon.

Summer.

Tango Delta

The lights come up on a rooftop of a tall building high above the business district of a large city.

Summer. Bright sunlight.

Three men on the roof. Agent One stands facing out front. He is a muscular, well-built man, probably somewhere in his thirties. He has a mustache. Wears a conservative business suit. Sunglasses. An earplug wire runs from his ear inside his jacket. His stance is alert, feet slightly apart. His face is impassive. He carries a walkie-talkie.

Agents Two and Three flank him on either side, facing off to the sides. Both wear suits similar to Agent One's. Also sunglasses. Earplugs and wires. Agent Two carries a rifle with a telescopic sight. He peers through it as he scans his view.

Agent Three is looking through high-powered binoculars. He never moves or shifts position.

As the lights come up, we hear the sound of radio static and an amplified male voice coming over the walkie-talkie.

VOICE: Tango Delta, five-niner. Tango Delta, five-niner, over.

AGENT ONE: *(Into walkie-talkie.)* Tango Delta. Home Port, over.

VOICE: Tango, are you in position, over?

AGENT ONE: Tango, Home Port, we are, over.

VOICE: Tango Delta, do you have Flipper in view? Repeat, do you have Flipper in view, over?

AGENT ONE: Negative, Home Port, motorcade not in view yet, over.

VOICE: Tango, motorcade will be coming into your view in eight minutes and twenty-six seconds, counting, over.

AGENT ONE: Roger, Home Port, Flipper in view at eight twenty-six and counting down, over.

VOICE: Roger, Tango Delta, we're over, check back in six, over and out.

AGENT ONE: Tango Delta, over and out.

(Radio crackle stops.)

AGENT TWO: (Looking through telescope.) Got a glint off that building, sir.

AGENT ONE: Repeat.

AGENT TWO: Got a glint off that building, sir. Reflection. Sun's in the wrong position.

AGENT ONE: Metallic?

AGENT TWO: Could be a gun barrel, sir.

AGENT ONE: Let it pass.

AGENT TWO: Sir?

AGENT ONE: You're seeing a reflection of a reflection. Picks up the sun's glare in reverse. Like a mirage in the desert.

AGENT TWO: Sorry, sir. Didn't mean to panic.

AGENT ONE: You have to keep on the alert. It was a good note. It was incorrect, but it was a good note.

AGENT TWO: Yes, sir.

AGENT ONE: (Into walkie-talkie.) Tango Pacific, this is Tango Delta, come in, over. Tango Pacific, this is Tango Delta, respond please, over.

VOICE: (Crackle.) Tango Delta, this is Tango Pacific, we copy, over.

AGENT ONE: Tango, are you taking the third quadrant at the overpass, over?

VOICE: Roger, Tango Delta, Team Seven is covering the overpass via the rooftop of the Episcopal Church at Lagoona Avenue. Ground teams taking street sweeps every half minute inside the two hundred yards, over.

AGENT ONE: Tango, we've got motorcade sighting in seven and counting, you're on follow-up at eight fifty-seven and down, over.

VOICE: Roger, Tango, we're right behind you, over.

AGENT ONE: Roger, Pacific, over and out.

AGENT TWO: Who's carrying the fourth quadrant, sir.

AGENT ONE: Tango Gulfstream's got everything below City Hall, but Home Port is going to use an alternate route through quadrant six at Kasky Parkway. They'll miss Gulfstream altogether. But they'll take the cue off us just in case. After the third pass of Flying-Fish Twelve.

AGENT TWO: (Points up.) There she is, sir. At two o'clock.

AGENT ONE: (Into walkie-talkie.) Tango Flying-Fish Twelve, this is Tango Delta, please respond. Tango Flying-Fish, this is Tango Delta, come in, over.

VOICE: *(Crackle and helicoper sounds.)* Roger, Delta, over.

AGENT ONE: Just checking in, Flying-Fish, have you got Flipper in your view, over?

VOICE: Affirmative, Delta, motorcade is fifteen seconds ahead of schedule, just passing the Mercantile Mart now, over.

AGENT ONE: Anything on the protest at the Commerce Building, over?

VOICE: No troubles, Delta, marchers and placards, some swearing, nothing of importance. Deep surveillance and photo ID covering the crowd, no reports, no worries, over.

AGENT ONE: Roger, Flying-Fish, we'll check back after our sighting, that in six, plus, coming down, over.

VOICE: Roger, Tango Delta, over and out.

AGENT TWO: I've got a figure at a window, sir.

AGENT ONE: Repeat.

AGENT TWO: A figure at a window. Black glass one. At one o'clock.

AGENT ONE: Right. That's one of the Para-Teams. He's taking position in that window. He's us. It was a change from headquarters. It was on the morning roster sheet. You didn't see the morning roster sheet?

AGENT TWO: Yes, sir.

AGENT ONE: You didn't see his position on the morning roster sheet?

AGENT TWO: No, sir.

AGENT ONE: You didn't check the morning roster sheet.

AGENT TWO: No, sir.

AGENT ONE: Well, he's one of us, so there's no reason to panic.

AGENT TWO: Sorry, sir.

AGENT ONE: This your first time on Flipper advance?

AGENT TWO: First time on roof surveillance. Never done an advance for "Flipper" before, sir. I worked a crowd control for one of the First Lady's speeches—

AGENT ONE: Use code.

AGENT TWO: Sir?

AGENT ONE: Use code.

AGENT TWO: I worked crowd control for a trip with Barracuda. This is the first time I've been on with Flipper *and* Barracuda.

AGENT ONE: I got two greenies today.

AGENT TWO: I worked a personal guard squad for the Secretary of the Treasury, sir.

AGENT ONE: Where at?

AGENT TWO: Kansas City, sir. FDIC Meeting. Three weeks ago.

AGENT ONE: On staff or training?

AGENT TWO: Training, sir.

AGENT ONE: Two greenies.

AGENT TWO: Yes, sir.

AGENT ONE: There's a shadow down there. Your quadrant. At seven o'clock. It's a deep shadow middle of the street between the Post Office Building and the Library Steps. You could run a paramilitary group down that street under that shadow and we wouldn't be able to see them from here till it was too late. Not with the sun reflecting in our eyes that way.

AGENT TWO: Shall I call it into Home Port, sir?

AGENT ONE: No. It belongs to Tango Coastal Point. But keep an eye on it.

AGENT TWO: Yes, sir.

AGENT ONE: There are no trees.

AGENT TWO: Sir?

AGENT ONE: No trees in this area. Mid-town…warehouse district…expressway…government buildings… park…concrete park. Not a tree in sight. Not even in the concrete park. Got no trees in our quadrant.

AGENT TWO: No, sir. We don't, sir.

AGENT ONE: No trees, no shade, no boughs, not a branch. Not a tree in sight. *(Beat.)* I hate trees.

AGENT TWO: Sir?

AGENT ONE: Trees. I hate 'em. Trees are good cover for snipers.

AGENT TWO: Yes, sir.

AGENT ONE: Grassy knolls.

AGENT TWO: Yes, sir. Sir?

AGENT ONE: Grassy Knoll. November twenty-second, 1963. 12:10 PM, Eastern Standard Time. Deeley Plaza. Dallas.

AGENT TWO: Yes, sir.

AGENT ONE: Zapruder film. Man with the umbrella. Grassy knoll. Man at the tree on the grassy knoll. I hate grassy knolls.

AGENT TWO: I always thought a grassy knoll sounded kind of … bucolic.

AGENT ONE: Yeah, it's bucolic. I hate bucolic. Too many places for an assassin to hide in "bucolic."

AGENT TWO: Yes, sir. *(Beat.)* Sir, I hate pastoral scenes, sir.

AGENT ONE: Well, that's good. Grassy knoll sounds pretty. Sounds like a pretty place. Place where you take your spoken-for or your fiancée. Place where you go for a picnic. Breezy day. Honeysuckle and heather. Wind in the grass like waves on a sea. And when the bough breaks, the cradle will fall.

AGENT TWO: Yes, sir. Kind of like an impressionist painting, sir.

AGENT ONE: I hate impressionism.

AGENT TWO: Me, too, sir.

AGENT ONE: Sit with your spoken-for, your lady-beloved. Drop a 30/30 across the branch, etch the notch, fix the sight, pull the trigger. Grassy Knoll. Pastoral as all damn hell.

AGENT TWO: Sir?

AGENT ONE: Yes.

AGENT TWO: I got a car on Bryant Avenue, moving south-southwest in the turning lane into Kasky Parkway. Supposed to be a cleared street sir.

AGENT ONE: *(Into walkie-talkie.)* Tango Home Port, this is Tango Delta, over. Tango Home Port, this is Tango Delta, do you read, over?

VOICE: Copy, Delta, this is Home Port, over?

AGENT ONE: We have a vehicle on Bryant Avenue moving south-southwest into Kasky Parkway. This is a cleared area, over.

VOICE: Roger, Tango Delta, that's plainclothes city police, unmarked, moving into position, they're three minutes behind schedule. All is well, over.

AGENT ONE: Just wanted to double-check, Home Port, Tango Delta over and out.

VOICE: Thanks for thinking of us, out.

AGENT ONE: *(After a pause, a kind of sigh.)* Bidda-*bee*-bidda-*boo*-bidda-*ba*. *(Pause.)* You ever worked a close-contact heavy crowd-control before?

AGENT TWO: No, sir. Just top surveillance and back-up for lower level administration officers, sir.

AGENT ONE: Two of the toughest jobs in the Service. Workin' a crowd, tryin' to pick out the killers...and standin' on top of a building watching for snipers.

AGENT TWO: Yes, sir.

AGENT ONE: No in-between. No matter where you go. Convention where they love the man, fans at the Western White House, speech in his home state, visit to his old high school...nobody's not a suspicious character; they're all guilty until proven innocent. You're standin' there, you're lookin', you're revolvin', your eyes are trackin' them. Each one of them has a gun. Every one. Every eye. Every face. Every smile. Every hand out to get a touch or a grasp of the man. Everybody's a killer. You gotta look into their faces and think, "Which one of them's gonna pull the trigger today?" Which one and why? Why would they kill *him?* Maybe they lost their job, maybe their business is failing, maybe they had a bad childhood, no one'll publish their book, they never let you play basketball after school, you got beat up in a bar one night because you said you wanted to watch *Masterpiece Theater* on the TV, your car doesn't get good mileage, your parents think you're gay, your wife's just left you, you can't get married in a lesbian church, the bus never seems to want to let you off at your stop even though you rang the bell five times, you never learned French, you can't pronounce certain vegetables, you always got picked last for volleyball, your house always got soaped and toilet-papered more than anyone else's on Halloween, you're fat, you're skinny, you're bald, you got a bad face problem, you don't get enough fiber, you're behind payments on the mobile home, you still say "groovy," your tie is too wide, I missed the state lottery by one number, my brother could buy and sell me, had a pimple on my nose night of the prom, my socks keep falling down, I should have bought gas when I saw I was on empty, I left my keys in the car, did I leave the stove on, why can't I type a résumé, why are the pay phones I try to use always out of order, I always miss the "Chuckles the Clown" episode on *Mary Tyler Moore* reruns, I never saw *My Fair Lady* on Broadway, you look at them, you look at them, you look at them, their faces, and then you say, "They're *all* guilty." And then you gotta figure which ones are gonna pull the trigger. You gotta put yourself in that position, you gotta say, "How *bad* does that affect me? How *bad* does havin' the car run out of gas affect me? How *bad* does missin' my favorite TV show affect me? How *bad* does bein' picked last for volleyball affect me? Why do I wanna blame him, why do I want to kill him, and then you think that you know, and you start to say, "I know why *I* would kill him!" And you hold onto your gun and you say, "Why do *I* get these assignments when all the others get the cushy duty ridin' in the backseat of the limos? Why do *I* have to stand on top of these goddamn roofs? And you say, "Yeah, I'd kill him, I'd shoot 'em, sure, right through the head, I'd shoot him!" *(Pause.)* Of course, this is just a technical exercise.

AGENT TWO: Yes, sir.

AGENT ONE: *(Pause.)* To, uh…to protect the man, you have to want to…to *kill* the man. In a way.

AGENT TWO: Sure.

AGENT ONE: Put…put yourself in…in…uhh…

(Beat.)

AGENT TWO: Yeah. Uh…sir.

AGENT ONE: You have to get inside the Other. You have to get inside. Think their way, be them. But not become them. Technical exercise. Turn it on. Turn it off. Click.

(Pause. Crackle of radio static.)

VOICE: Tango Delta, five-niner. Tango Delta, five-niner, over. *(Pause.)* Tango Delta, five-niner. Tango Delta, five-niner, over. *(Beat.)* Are you on, Tango? Can you hear me, Ted?

(Agent One jumps and hurriedly brings the walkie-talkie to his mouth.)

AGENT ONE: Yeah, I'm, uh, on, uh…Tango Delta, Home Port, I copy, over.

VOICE: Tango, you've got motorcade in thirty-three seconds and down, over.

AGENT ONE: Roger, Home Port, we're counting down from thirty, over.

(Sound of motorcade approaching. Engines, sirens, etc.)

VOICE: Flipper's got the bubble-top window down a few inches, problem with the A.C., over.

AGENT ONE: This heat'd cook him alive, Home Port, over.

VOICE: It makes him sleepy. You can just see his head nodding off through the window, over.

AGENT ONE: *(Peering through his binoculars.)* Yeah, Roger, Home Port, I got him now, nine seconds early, hundred and fifty yards, over.

VOICE: Roger, follow him through, he'll be out of view in twenty-one seconds, over.

AGENT ONE: Roger, Home Port, got him high and clear. High and clear. Click.

VOICE: Repeat that, Tango.

AGENT ONE: Uh…click. Nothing, Home Port, erase, over.

VOICE: Roger, Tango Delta, over and out.

(Agent One continues to peer through his binoculars to the end of the play.)

AGENT ONE: All right, we follow him through, till Flipper's out of sight in…eleven seconds, now at one hundred ten yards.

AGENT TWO: Yes, sir.

(Agent Two turns with his rifle and points it out front. He peers through the telescope.)

AGENT ONE: Eight seconds at ninety yards. Eighty yards. Seventy yards. There he is asleep in the backseat. Like a baby.

AGENT TWO: *(His finger on the trigger.)* I got him, sir.

AGENT ONE: High and clear. Click-click-click. Bidda-*bee*-bidda-*boo*-bidda-*ba*. So, where are you two from, huh?

AGENT TWO: *(Tugging on the trigger.)* Harkov, sir.

(Agent Three puts away his binoculars, takes a service revolver from his holster, and turns to Agent One.)

AGENT ONE: Don't know it. You?

AGENT TWO: He's from St. Petersburg.

AGENT ONE: Oh. Florida State?

AGENT TWO: Little farther east.

(Agent Three carefully takes aim and places the gun barrel behind Agent One's left ear.)

AGENT ONE: *(Still peering out front.)* Yeah? Hm. High and clear. Click-click-click.

(Agent Two is pulling his trigger. Agent Three is pulling his trigger. The motorcade is roaring now. Blackout.)

END OF PLAY

Seeing the Light
by Robert McKay

CHARACTERS
NED

MARSHALL

CASEY

Seeing the Light

Two men are seated at a table. One of the men, Marshall, is reading a paper or magazine. His feet are up on the table. The other man, Ned, is busy playing solitaire. Overhead, as if in the ceiling, is a light. It is not on when the lights come up. After a short time, in which Marshall is buried in his reading, and Ned is intent on his cards, the light comes on. It is red. Neither man notices the light. Finally, after some time, Ned sees that the light is on. He returns to his game, then his attention comes back to the light. He looks at it for a while, almost plays another card, looks back. It's still on. At this point, he speaks.

NED: Marshall. *(Marshall grunts.)* Marshall, look at that.

MARSHALL: *(Still buried.)* What?

NED: The light.

MARSHALL: *(Not coming out.)* What about the light, Ned?

NED: It's on. *(After a pause, with reluctance, and a show which reveals how little he likes being interrupted, Marshall takes a look. Yes, the light is on. Without comment, Marshall goes back to his reading.)* Marshall? *(Marshall grunts.)* Don't you think we should do something?

MARSHALL: *(From behind his paper.)* What do you think we should do, Ned?

NED: Tell somebody? Notify somebody?

MARSHALL: *(Looking at Ned around his reading.)* Who somebody, Ned?

NED: Uh—

MARSHALL: What are you gonna tell 'em, Ned?

NED: That the light's on.

(At this, Marshall does put down his reading.)

MARSHALL: You're going to tell somebody that the light's on.

NED: I thought we should.

MARSHALL: Because it's our job?

NED: Yeah. We're supposed to—

MARSHALL: We're supposed to use our judgment, Ned.

NED: The light's on, Marshall. Isn't it?

MARSHALL: You know it is, Ned.

NED: Then we're supposed to call.

MARSHALL: Simple as that, Ned, in all the time we've been here— How long have you been here, Ned?

NED: Almost fifteen years.

MARSHALL: Fifteen years. I've been here eighteen years, Ned. In all that time, have you ever seen the light go on?

NED: No.

MARSHALL: Not once?

NED: No.

MARSHALL: Not even a blink?

NED: No.

MARSHALL: Have you ever heard of the light going on?

NED: No.

MARSHALL: Not even once? Not one single time?

NED: No.

MARSHALL: OK.

NED: But—

MARSHALL: Now it's on.

NED: That's right.

MARSHALL: And what are you going to do? Are you going to come unglued, Ned? Lose your head? Go to pieces? All the training, all the trust that's been placed in you, and me, are you going to just toss that out the window and hit the panic button? Are you, Ned?

NED: *(Summoning his courage.)* I think we should call. *(Marshall shakes his head, disgusted. Ned becomes agitated.)* Don't you? What do you think we should do, Marshall? Because the light is on. It's definitely on. It's—on.

MARSHALL: I can see the light, Ned.

NED: OK.

MARSHALL: The question, now that the light is on, is what do we do about it.

NED: OK.

MARSHALL: Now the fact that the light is on can mean, I think, as I run over the possibilities in my mind, one of two things. If you think of any other possibilities, Ned, just jump right in, OK?

NED: OK.

MARSHALL: Possibility Number One: The light is defective. Meaning: There is no crisis.

NED: Boy, I don't see how that's possible, Marshall.

MARSHALL: It's like in your car, Ned. Happened to me last month. I'm drivin' along, all of a sudden this light comes on: "Check engine." Oh Mamma, I thought my car was gonna blow up. I pulled over as fast as I could and called the dealer. Talked to a mechanic. "This light just came on!" Know what he did, Ned? He laughed! Said it happens all the time, sooner or later. Doesn't mean a thing. Nothin's wrong with the engine, the light's busted. All I hadda do was pull the fuse. No more light. Next time I take it in, they'll fix it. Car runs fine. Saved myself worry, aggravation, all that time, a couple hundred bucks. You see what I'm sayin'? Could be the same situation we got right here.

NED: How do you know that?

MARSHALL: We don't. I'm saying it's a possibility. Ned, I'm saying it should be checked before we turn weapons of mass destruction loose. Maybe we should check the bulb before we unleash Armageddon. Don't you think we should do that?

NED: I guess so. *(Pause.)* How do we check the light?

MARSHALL: I'm not sure.

NED: Marshall, this isn't like your car. Do you know how many fail-safe systems are supporting this light? They've got redundancy piled on redundancy, backups on the backups, all to make sure this light works. And now—now—

MARSHALL: In the first place, Ned, let me remind you: To err is human. OK?

NED: OK.

MARSHALL: Secondly, if humans can err, think about governments. Humans make mistakes. Governments are mistakes. Think about all those glorious hi-tech systems they've built to insure that this one crummy little light cannot fail. OK? Now I ask you: What have they done? They've just increased their chances for error, that's all. In fact, if you think about it, they've put so much work into this one light that they've practically guaranteed a screwup. It's inevitable. It's like any government system, Ned. It gets so big and complicated that it gets stupid. They ever make a mistake on your paycheck?

NED: Sure.

MARSHALL: Screw up your vacation time?

NED: Yeah.

MARSHALL: Spell your name wrong?

NED: *(Brightening.)* All the time.

MARSHALL: You see?

(There is a euphoric pause while they reflect on this happy news. Marshall returns to his reading.)

NED: Marshall? *(Marshall grunts.)* What is the second possibility?

MARSHALL: *(From behind reading.)* That the light isn't broken.

NED: *(Wetting his lips.)* And we're really under attack?

MARSHALL: That's right.

NED: My God.

MARSHALL: *(Comes out to face Ned.)* Exactly.

NED: What?

MARSHALL: Prayer, Ned. A moment with your Maker. Forget about making a call. If that light is working, I suggest you get down on your knees.

NED: That's not in the manual.

MARSHALL: Screw the manual, Ned. If that light isn't broken—

NED: I know.

MARSHALL: What are we talking about? The sky dark with nuclear missiles? The lucky ones die in the blast. The survivors experience the effects of global radioactive contamination. Or maybe it's not bombs. Maybe it's biochem, anthrax, ricin, sarin—choose your poison, Ned.

NED: No.

MARSHALL: And what would happen if we did follow the book? Panic. And what kind of a response would we get? Chaos. Bickering over what to do. Interagency quarrels, interdepartmental breakdowns, isolated power grabs, all the top leaders heading for cover, in bunkers, leaving the rest of us to—

NED: Stop. No more.

MARSHALL: That's the second possibility, Ned. You asked me. You want estimates on the initial casualties?

NED: No.

MARSHALL: Fifty million, minimum. That's before retaliation, of course. Which comes as a direct result of our response to the light.

NED: *(A final desperate plea.)* Don't you think we should call?

(There is a pause while they consider this. Casey enters.)

CASEY: Hey, guys.

MARSHALL: Casey. Look at this.

CASEY: *(Sees the light.)* Whoa.

MARSHALL: What do you think?

CASEY: Maybe it's broken.

MARSHALL: That's what I've been trying to tell him. He wants to call.

CASEY: Hoo, I don't know about that. You make that call—

MARSHALL: That's right.

CASEY: That's serious. You start a chain reaction—

MARSHALL: Yowza. Get the picture, Ned?

NED: But it's our job to notify them if the light goes on.

CASEY: No, it isn't.

NED: How do you figure?

CASEY: Look, if they wanted it like that, Ned, they'd make the whole system automatic. There'd be no delay whatsoever. Those circuits ever fire up, boom, we'd launch, automatic, instantaneous, everything we've got.

MARSHALL: We're here to prevent that.

NED: You're saying we do nothing? No matter what?

> *(Pause.)*

CASEY: Say, I'm going out for sandwiches. You guys want anything?

MARSHALL: I'll have smoked turkey with mayo and onion.

CASEY: Lettuce on that?

MARSHALL: No.

CASEY: Bun?

MARSHALL: Kaiser.

NED: I don't believe you guys! The world—the whole world could be—

CASEY: You want a sandwich or not?

NED: *(Pauses, gives in.)* Hard salami, tomato, lettuce on whole wheat.

CASEY: Mayo?

NED: No, I'm trying to cut down.

CASEY: OK. I'll be back.

> *(Casey exits. Marshall goes back to his reading. Ned stares at the light. Ned gets on his knees and prays. Gets back in his chair, looking at the light. Begins to pick up and shuffle his cards. The light goes off. He doesn't see this, then notices it.)*

NED: Hey! Marshall!

> *(Marshall grunts.)*

NED: Nothing.

> *(Ned resumes his game. The light begins to blink. Ned jumps behind his chair, stares at it. To black.)*

END OF PLAY

Plays
for
Three Women

Eating Out
by Marcia Dixcy

CHARACTERS

CHRISS: Twenties, very thin, an anorexic.

MELANIE: Twenties, medium build, a bulimic.

PAT: Late twenties, an all-American girl.

SETTING

Very simple. Each woman sits in a spotlight. Each may have a small table beside her, if you wish. Pat may smoke.

Eating Out

CHRISS: I haven't always been thin. People just assume that. They assume that I'm lucky. I can eat anything I want while they just have to look at food to put on weight. I feel like saying, "Obviously you're doing a lot more than looking." And I...can't even imagine eating anything I'd want. Kind of makes me sick to think of it. When I was in high school, all I wanted to be was petite and blonde. Instead, I was dark, dark and skinny and intense. I have one high school picture where I look exactly like something out of Aubrey Beardsley. So that was my persona, at least until I got to college. There, the world began to change. And I was reading anything that would make sense out of it. Every week, a new philosophy. Somewhere between Existentialism and Phenomenology, I guess I began to lose faith. Structures began to give way; decisions became more complex. Anyway, eating became an important comfort—a communal obsession. One true thing about women's college is the freshman ton. Collectively, every freshman class of 250 gains a ton. And that's probably a low estimate. So, I didn't play tennis, and I wasn't really in the ballpark with some of the incredible brains, and pretty soon, I wasn't even skinny anymore. Sex? *(Laughs.)* You know, I was so God damned scared. Let's not even talk about losing my virginity. First time out, I got vaginal warts. So I thought, forget it. This is just too much pain, too much pain. So, it was about that time, about the time when large gray areas began to overpower the black and whites, that I embarked on my first real diet. And I was very serious. I made a serious list: no fats, no fried foods, no pizza, no desserts, no bread, no cookies—my entire food intake up to that point. And of course a diet like that would work. You know, the Behaviorists say there's an optimum schedule for positive reinforcement so that you can train animals or humans to do anything. So, I guess that's what I did. That's how I trained myself to starve.

MELANIE: There are always rituals. The days you get through and the days you know you'll probably eat. Not meals. I almost never eat a meal. These rituals are alone, and they're usually late—later than you'd want a meal. Sometimes just at the point when you think you might go to bed—

without. And usually, you pretend it'll just be one thing, and that will be all. But from that moment on, it seems open-ended and nothing stops it. The telephone can ring, the doorbell—you just get rid of them. Because you're racing, and you don't want to be interrupted. If you have to wait too long for the toaster, you start on cereal: bowl after bowl, and then from the box. 'Course, you have to undo your clothes—forget the jeans. Pretty soon, you take them off and cover yourself with something huge. You know, like those dogs that have the big collars around their necks that stick out about a foot so they can't bite at some hurt they have? You just divorce your body. You separate your mouth from it. And your mouth can go on forever.

PAT: I've tried it all: fasting, puking, laxatives, jogging, aerobics; it's a full-time job. I suppose the next thing will be plastic surgery, liposuction. From what I've read that'll be the wave of the future. And I remember my grandmother telling me that her mother seriously considered having her two lowest ribs removed so she could cinch her corset in tighter. Apparently, there was really a craze for that. So, some things just don't improve. But there are ways to make it easier. Some you can live with, and—some you can't. And I remember the best, really the best for me was in capsule form. It's virtually impossible now, but seven or eight years ago you could still manage to get Control II drugs. At that time I had met a medical student and he knew this resident and we worked out a cooperative system. The resident would write me a prescription. You see, they needed me because they said it would be most unusual for these diet pills to be prescribed for a man. Seems strange, since those doctors really thrived on 'em—particularly mixed with alcohol. But Norman, this medical student, and I would drive outside the city—I was in college in Washington, DC—and we would find these smallish towns and I would go in and get the drugs: biamphetamines, they were called. Black beauties. The first time I had one was on a Sunday: a biamphetamine brunch. And to this day, I remember that afternoon, the intensity and the power. The power to keep on going—without sleep, without food. We took this marathon bike ride. I don't even like bike-riding, really, 'cause the cars drive me crazy. But on the speed, it felt like I could pedal right off the earth, right off the rim of the horizon. And it was over forty-eight hours before I ate anything.

CHRISS: I had elaborate strategies to keep myself from eating. One more hour, make it through one more hour, and then the next. When I did eat, it was always exactly at the same time of day—my entire life had to be organized around that. And I always ate exactly the same things. Lettuce—large platefuls of lettuce, broth, vegetables—raw vegetables, and hard-boiled eggs—sometimes just the whites. I read somewhere that hard-boiled eggs had less calories in them than they took to digest, and, combined with grapefruit, they could actually metabolize fat. *(Laughs.)* Eventually, I ate all my meals up in my room. Alone.

MELANIE: Part of the deal is you keep drinking water and you keep alternating things. Like the cereal, the granola, which is sweet. I eat that in and out with bagels, bagels with Muenster cheese, lettuce, and mayonnaise. The whole time, I always keep track of the calories in everything. They're on the package, or the box, or on the bag of bagels. Since the mayonnaise is by the tablespoon, and I don't exactly use a whole tablespoon every time, I figure, you know, just let it go. But when you finish almost a whole box of granola and three or four bagel cheese deals, we're talking thousands of calories. It gets kind of surreal. You feel—superhuman—I don't know.

PAT: For awhile, I only took one, once a week. I'd get wiped out, depleted for a few days after. I mean, it's like the adrenaline is coursing through your body, probably burning up about twice the calories. And the weight just really dropped off.

CHRISS: I weighed myself constantly, but since I was drinking so much water and Tab, I was always one or two pounds heavier than I wanted to be. First it was 125, then 115. Then I had to work a little harder so I took up swimming. I swam late in the afternoon before dinner because when I got out of the water, I knew that would be the point in the day when I weighed the very least. And every ounce I lost encouraged me to eat that much less.

MELANIE: By that time, it's all really expanding in your stomach, which is totally distended, pretty uncomfortable. And then, you start thinking about how to soothe it. I guess what you'd call the classic cure is Häagen Dazs ice cream. Anyone knows how fast a pint of that can go. Long as you got that mental collar round your neck, it goes right down.

PAT: Pretty soon it actually got kind of difficult to buy the pills. By that time, I had lost about twenty pounds. It was in the summer, you see. So we'd have to wait until a rainy day and I could wear a big slicker thing with a lot of sweat shirts under it so nobody would see my body. Still, the pharmacists who did fill the prescription for weight loss had to figure something was screwy. I thought I looked good. But my friends—one of them told me later that my face looked like a skull. Bone and skin. It was what I'd always fantasized about. That and dating a doctor.

CHRISS: My clothes became a kind of joke—huge clown pants which I'd belt in way above my waist. I went to try on other clothes. Any clothes that fit me made me feel—fat. In the dressing rooms, I always felt so discouraged. One doctor later told me that sometimes people are trapped inside the wrong bodies. They have no idea what body they really have. There are thin people who're trapped in fat bodies and they'll wear anything—tight jeans, whatever, because in their minds they look terrific. But I was just the opposite. I was a fat person trapped in a thin body. And no matter what anyone said, no matter what I weighed, or how sharp my hip bones protruded through my skin…or my vertebrae, or my ribs, no matter how delicate my wrist, I would always be too fat.

MELANIE: With ice cream you need something warm, to kind of melt it. Tea, maybe peppermint tea. Next you want something salty; popcorn, if you're desperate, or chips, if you've thought ahead. Maybe dip. Then it depends on what's around—chocolate, something from the freezer, you know, biscuits, or spinach soufflé, or pound cake. You might not even wait for it to thaw.

PAT: I felt like I'd discovered a new twist on the fountain of youth: a prescription substitute for nourishment and sleep. So why wasn't everybody taking it? Pretty soon I was up to a pill every other day, eating and sleeping half as much as the rest of the world. What I found out was all this extra energy didn't come in the capsule. The speed just releases certain chemicals stored up in your body and supplies of those are limited. To put it simply, whatever chemical my nervous system needed to transmit its messages got used up. And I knew I was really going haywire. For one thing, I got the chronic shakes. It became impossible to sit still in almost any situation. So I started not showing up for stuff. I think people began to find me pretty weird and unpredictable. Finally, one day, I bit right through my lower lip—bit a hole right through the middle of it.

CHRISS: It was a year before I told anyone that I'd stopped menstruating. That just seemed a blessing.

MELANIE: I wish I was exaggerating. I often think about my mother, or God, or whoever might be watching. And it's like there you are, stepping off some kind of cliff, and you do it because you know it isn't real. No one else is out there. And tomorrow, it'll all be gone.

PAT: That was that, man. I took the last bottle of pills and dumped it. Norman was really pissed at me later, but at that point, I just wanted them gone. It was a week before I could really sleep. Then, I was out for days. Afterwards it was like reentry into the normal world. Nothing felt quite the same, no instant enthusiasm. And the weight, you know at first, it was fun to gain a little back, but then it was the same old drag.

CHRISS: What finally happened was I went to give blood. You know, "A pint's a pound the world around." What I didn't know was that to give a pint of blood, you have to weigh 110 pounds. I was pretty far below that…I weighed 94. And there were other things. I was always freezing and there was this hair growth—this facial hair. It all got kind of out of my control.

MELANIE: I always know, because I've always checked, exactly what I weighed before, what I weighed even an hour ago. Sometimes, I've gained as much as ten pounds, sometimes more. I have a big plastic bowl. I keep it under the sink with the sponges and disinfectants there. I take it into the bathroom and set it right on my scale. And, I get on my hands and knees, I mean you know what way *you* have to do it. But I guess, at first, it pretty much has to be your fingers, at least for most people. At some point, you can train yourself and then, it's just a matter of muscle control.

PAT: There've been a few times since then, I've bought those over-the-counter diet pills. But no. They're just massive caffeine and a stomachache. They don't really tempt me. No, it's hard.

MELANIE: It can go like crazy at first. I mean, ice cream is easy, but other things, like chocolate, are really harder, and—it's willpower then. But I won't stop until the scale is right—exactly the right weight—give or take whatever for the bowl. So, I fill it up until I'm rid of it, completely rid of it. And then it's over. So, I can wash the bowl, take a shower, and go to bed.

CHRISS: But that's the thing about control. When you lose it, you realize how hard it is to get it back and when you get it back, the most frightening thing in the world is the thought of ever losing it again.

MELANIE: When I go out to dinner, I can start to feel this panic. I mean, I try to avoid it if it ever comes up—even with my family.

PAT: I like the procedure where they wire your mouth shut. Sort of like braces to straighten out your self-control.

CHRISS: I often say I've just eaten a huge lunch. People tend to feel guilty if I tell them I'm dieting.

PAT: Otherwise, you're stuck with the same old excuses.

MELANIE: It's my stomach—really giving me trouble today.

PAT: I'm cleaning my system with fluids.

CHRISS: No, I'm allergic to animal fat.

MELANIE: Basically, I'm a vegetarian.

PAT: I'm too wound up to eat right now.

MELANIE: I'll have something later when I get home.

CHRISS: I could just have a bite of yours.

PAT: You go ahead, I'll enjoy it.

CHRISS: But, I'm really not that hungry.

PAT: And, I'm really not that hungry.

MELANIE: 'Cause, I'm really not that hungry.

END OF PLAY

The Office
by Kate Hoffower

for Robin, Jeanette and Jillian

The Office was first produced in a staged reading at Chicago Dramatists.

CHARACTERS
ONE
TWO
THREE

TIME
The present.

The Office

Lights up as an unassuming customer service representative enters (Three). She is normal looking, on the bland side. She takes a seat at the upstage center desk and begins to shuffle papers. She does not speak, but works quietly at her desk throughout the play. She is rarely acknowledged by One and Two but observes them carefully. Blackout.

Lights up on One and Two slumped in their chairs and/or sprawled across their desks downstage left and right. Their eyes are filled with infinite vacuity.

ONE: I'm bored.

TWO: Me too.

ONE: I've never been this bored.

TWO: Me neither.

ONE: Never in my entire life.

TWO: Never. Not this bored.

ONE: I'm beyond bored.

TWO: I'm *beyond* beyond bored.

ONE: I'm beyond *being* beyond—

TWO: bored.

ONE: I'm—

TWO: so bored.

ONE: So very, very, very—

TWO: bored.

ONE AND TWO: I

ONE AND TWO: am

ONE AND TWO: so

ONE AND TWO: *bored.*

ONE: *(Stuffing a pencil in her ear.)* What time is it?

TWO: *(Stuffing a pencil in her ear.)* Nine AM.

ONE: *(Stuffing a pencil in her nose.)* What time is it now?

TWO: *(Stuffing a pencil in her nose.)* Nine AM and three seconds.

ONE: *(Stuffing her remaining nasal and aural orifices with pencils.)* Now?

TWO: *(Likewise.)* Nine AM and four of the most boring seconds I have ever experienced in my *life*.

ONE: Never

TWO: ever

ONE: have

TWO: I

ONE: ever

TWO: been

ONE: this

ONE AND TWO: BORED!

ONE: If I have pretzels on my desk today, and he comes by and eats them again without asking, I'm going to punch him.

TWO: Tell him that's all you can afford to bring for lunch on the miserable salary he pays you, and if he doesn't keep his hands *off*, you'll have him arrested.

ONE: If he fires me how much can I collect in unemployment?

TWO: Probably more than you're making now. Hey—have you ever noticed that sometimes when he's standing over your desk talking *at* you that he sort of reaches down and smooths the front of his pants…*excessively?*

ONE: Yes! But it's more like he's patting himself—trying to calm himself down.

TWO: It seems pretty sick to me.

ONE: Maybe it's just a habit.

TWO: Yeah. Maybe when he was a kid his parents wouldn't let him have a pet. So instead of a dog or a cat—

ONE: He started petting *himself!*

ONE AND TWO: Aghhhh!!!!!!

TWO: If only he wasn't looking over my shoulder constantly—if he was just here part-time it wouldn't be so bad.

ONE: Yeah, well, good luck. He already works like two hundred hours a week.

TWO: He'd have to cut down if he had a heart attack.

ONE: Great. I'll sneak up behind him and yell boo.

TWO: No. I'm serious. Think about it. The average person burns about two thousand calories a day. And you have to eat thirty-five hundred calories more than you burn in order to gain a pound. He's fairly sedentary, and he doesn't work out or anything. —And I know he easily eats at least two thousand calories a day already. So if we could just get him to eat a little more and gain what? About fifty pounds? Would that do it?

ONE: I don't know. It would help I guess.

TWO: OK. So how long would it take him to gain that much?

ONE: *(Hesitantly.)* Well, thirty-five hundred calories times fifty pounds is… *(She uses her calculator.)* a hundred seventy-five thousand extra calories. If he ate—let's say an extra five hundred calories a day—that's like two extra candy bars—it would take—

TWO: A hundred seventy-five thousand calories?

ONE: Yeah.

TWO: OK. A hundred seventy-five thousand calories divided by five hundred is—

ONE: Three hundred and fifty days.

TWO: Almost a year. But maybe it would take less than fifty pounds if we could add more stress to his life.

ONE: Yeah…but how would we get him to eat the extra two candy bars a day in the first place?

TWO: It wouldn't have to be candy bars. I could bring in donuts every once in a while. You could bring in cookies now and then. And there's always holiday food!

ONE: But what if it works? What if we kill him and get arrested for murder?

TWO: We couldn't get arrested. We didn't *make* him eat it. Besides, he'll probably just have a mild heart attack and have to cut down his work week. That would be perfect.

ONE: I guess so. *(Changing the subject.)* So whadja watch last night?

TWO: Sunday movie. You?

ONE: I went to bed early.

TWO: You always go to bed early.

ONE: You always go home and watch TV.

TWO: No. Sometimes I go home and watch TV and read *People* magazine and eat ice cream. All at the same time. *(Pause.)*

ONE: Jesus! Why are we still *here?*

TWO: I don't know.

ONE: I can remember being twelve years old and having my life completely planned out. I was going to graduate from the Eastman School of Music, sing professionally until I was twenty-six, get married, have two children, and then work part-time—*if* I felt like it.

TWO: Yikes!

ONE: Well, *you* can't have dreamt of a career in customer service.

TWO: No.

ONE: No. *(Pause.)*

TWO: I was going to be a brain surgeon. *(Three laughs. One and Two both turn to look at her. Three quickly returns to work.)*

ONE: A *brain* surgeon?

TWO: Yes! I remember watching cartoons one Saturday morning and seeing this commercial for some doll, and all these little girls in pink dresses were sitting around, very well behaved, brushing its hair, practically melting with sweetness. And the next ad was a bunch of boys skating through a fantasy world of castles and dragons, yelling and screaming and having the time of their lives. And then the very next ad was for that same stupid pink doll! So I told my Mom about it and she said, "That's because girls are supposed to sit at home and have babies, and boys are supposed to go out and have a whole hell of a lot of fun and not worry about anything." So I said, "Well I don't want to sit around and have babies. I want to have fun too." And she said, "Great. Be a brain surgeon."

ONE: She said, "Great. Be a brain surgeon?"

TWO: She said, "Great. Be a brain surgeon."

ONE: And?

TWO: And I took her seriously. I went to the library and started researching the brain. But then I started having trouble with math and science. I practically failed high school. And I eventually gave up med school dreams for art…. I've done some fantastic pastels of the temporal lobe.

ONE: My Dad called me last night. It really scared me because he never calls, so I figured something must be wrong. I couldn't believe it was him. He said, "Are you OK?" And I said, "I'm fine, why?" And he said, "I just got a feeling that something was wrong and I wanted to call." And suddenly I thought—yes, Dad. Something *is* wrong. I want to be a singer. I've dreamt about it my entire life but somehow I've ended up here. I work for seven-fifty an hour. I file, I answer phones, and I photocopy eight-and-a-half hours a day, forty-two-and-a-half hours a week, and every minute of every day my soul rots away just a little bit more. I'm twenty-eight years old and I'm dying. I'm already dead. I might as well be. I wanted to say, "Make me seven years old again Daddy. Stand with me on the top of the diving board and hold my hand as I look a million miles down at the long black arrows on the bottom of the pool. Then squeeze my hand and tell me that everything is going to be OK. We're just going to count to three and jump." *(Pause.)*

TWO: Take your bra off.

ONE: What!?

TWO: I dare you to take your bra off and wear it outside your clothes.

ONE: No! Why?

TWO: It will be a break from the monotony of our otherwise tedious and meaningless lives.

ONE: No!

TWO: I'll let you have the good stapler.

ONE: No.

TWO: I'll change the fax paper for you from now on.

ONE: *No.*

TWO: I'll teach you how to use Quark.

ONE: No…

TWO: Quark Xpress, version three point three one. I'll teach you how to set tabs, create master guides, and kern. You will learn how to make entries into the auxiliary dictionary, how to start a new library, and how to import text from Microsoft Word. I can teach you framing, modifying, and how to establish a baseline grid.

ONE: Will you teach me how to use the horizontal/vertical scale?

TWO: Yes!

ONE: OK, OK. I'll do it. But *you* have to do it too.

TWO: Why?

ONE: Because if you do, I'll agree to the heart attack thing. I'll start my part tomorrow by bringing in two dozen double chocolate donuts.

TWO: His favorite!

ONE: Exactly.

TWO: OK. Deal.

ONE: All right then. On your mark—

TWO: Get set—

ONE: Go! *(They both take off their bras underneath their shirts and rehook them on top. There can be some ad-libbing, ouches, and laughter. Three watches for a moment then silently joins them. They do not notice her. Three sits back down at her desk and resumes work while One and Two finish.)*

ONE: He's going to be here any minute.

TWO: He probably won't even notice!

ONE: He'll probably take one look and start rubbing himself like crazy.

ONE AND TWO: Aggghhhh!!!!!! *(They laugh again and return to their desks. Pause. They begin looking for something to do.)*

TWO: I am really bored.

ONE: Yep. Really, really bored.
TWO: Really
ONE: Really
TWO: *Really*
ONE: Bored.
    (Lights fade to black.)

END OF PLAY

Heads
by Jon Jory

CHARACTERS

MARGARET

KRISTEN

ROSE

Heads

Scene: A college dormitory represented by a bed, chair, night table, and bureau. Kristen is packing and Margaret is studying a script.

MARGARET: "Why look you now, how unworthy a thing you would make of me! You would play upon me, you would seem to know my stops, you would pluck out the heart of my mystery, you would sound me from my lowest note to the top of my compass. S'Blood, do you think I am easier to be played on than a pipe?"

KRISTEN: Hamlet, right?

MARGARET: Right.

KRISTEN: How come you always learn boys' parts?

MARGARET: 'Cause they've got all the best lines. You know what women do in plays? Fall in love, get seduced, commit suicide, and listen to men say all the best lines. I can't believe you're going.

KRISTEN: I would have been the first one in my family to get a master's.

MARGARET: You're really going to cut hair?

KRISTEN: Side by side with my daddy.

MARGARET: How come he won't stake you?

KRISTEN: Hasn't got it.

MARGARET: I thought all barbers were rich.

KRISTEN: Stylists are rich, barbers cut hair in Plenty Wood, Montana. Invite me to the wedding, will you?

MARGARET: Cross my heart. *(They embrace.)*

KRISTEN: What's it going to be like?

MARGARET: The best you can get for under a hundred dollars.

KRISTEN: Day-old cake.

MARGARET: A double pop-top ceremony.

(The door opens and a third young woman, Rose, enters.)

MARGARET: Yikes.

ROSE: Sit down.

KRISTEN: Scared me to death! You're white as a sheet.

ROSE: Sit down. Shut up.

KRISTEN: Nice talk.

MARGARET: Your mother didn't tell you not to interrupt a conversation?

ROSE: I found a wallet.

MARGARET: Yeah?

KRISTEN: So?

ROSE: In the dorm parking lot.

MARGARET: Rose, you could make a sunny day sound like a clue in a Hardy Boys' mystery. You suffer from congenital implication.

ROSE: Have we got any beer left?

MARGARET: Over there.

ROSE: It was right by my car. Right by it. God meant us to have this wallet.

MARGARET: So what's to be so hyped up about?

KRISTEN: A lot of money? What?

ROSE: Sit.

KRISTEN: I have to pack.

ROSE: Sit!

MARGARET: I thought you didn't drink beer?

ROSE: This wallet belongs to Teddy Leonard.

KRISTEN: Who?

MARGARET: That little pipsqueak guy? The one who stands around Pepito's by himself, reading Alfred North Whitehead so you'll know he's serious?

KRISTEN: From Joanie's class?

MARGARET: About this high. If you held him up to the light, he'd be transparent.

KRISTEN: The one she went out with that time? Splurged her to a hundred-dollar French dinner, and then dragged her to some documentary film on laser technology?

ROSE: Right.

KRISTEN: Too shy to talk to her?

ROSE: That's the one.

KRISTEN: So?

ROSE: Read this. *(She pulls a clipping out of the wallet and hands it to Kristen. Rose goes to get another beer.)*

KRISTEN: *(Impressed.)* No damn kidding! *(She hands the clipping to Margaret.)*

MARGARET: So tell me?

ROSE: Read it!

MARGARET: *(Reading.)* This can't be right. The kid dresses like a Republican president. I mean he's okay, but just kind of a nebbish. *(Kristen takes the clipping back.)*

KRISTEN: His daddy invented frozen orange juice.

ROSE: The nebbish is an only child. He's the heir to a couple of billion.

KRISTEN: *(Resuming her packing.)* Well, good for him. Maybe he'll be able to get a date.

ROSE: We're the only ones who know.

MARGARET: Listen, his secret is safe with me. Don't slurp the beer, okay? I have to study. *(She begins to read.)*

ROSE: Any one of us could have him.

MARGARET: I'm afraid I'd get cut by his braces.

ROSE: I'm not kidding.

KRISTEN: Kidding? Kidding? What is this, a movie about 1940s chorus girls?

ROSE: Think about it. Don't put a label on it. Think about it.

MARGARET: So you're serious?

ROSE: Serious! The will's probably in probate. That means in maybe thirteen months he has two billion dollars. Have you ever watched him? Always alone, and doing what?

MARGARET: You writing a thesis on this guy?

ROSE: What does he do all the time? *All* the time?

KRISTEN: Wears herringbone sports coats.

ROSE: Stares at women. This kid is sexually desperate. He's twenty years old and he's been too shy all his life. One hundred to one he has never touched one. Worse than that, he wants one imponderable thing. He wants to be loved for himself. If anyone finds out he's rich, it will never, never, ever happen. He wants someone to love him for the nebbish he is.

MARGARET: Okay, so take him.

ROSE: I don't need him. I'll be a pediatric allergist, remember, a doctor. People marry *me* for money. Plus I have the trust fund. Plus I have doting parents. Plus I'm driving a Corvette.

MARGARET: Congratulations. You have just won our "let them eat cake" award. Have another beer.

ROSE: I am giving him to you. Me. The goose who lays the golden eggs. Savvy? Blink your eyes twice if you catch my drift. *(They look at her.)* I ain't kidding, roomies. This is one of those moments that can change your life. We're the only ones who know. We call him up; he comes over; we're nice to him. He asks you out. You go. Again he asks. Again you go. You take your time. Maybe after two months you do some heavy petting. Instant marriage proposal!

MARGARET: Yuk, Rose, yuk.

KRISTEN: Deepest India. I mean, really. Listen, if he dies, do I have to throw myself on his funeral pyre?

ROSE: Thousands of millions. Unimaginable bucks. Stack it in tens it would fill the Astrodome. The interest income would be over…who knows? You want to be an actress? Produce the film. Hire Robert Redford. You want barbers? Buy a couple of hundred. Remember the law school you can't pay for? How about Harvard? Buy a house in Cambridge. Live-in help. Vacation in Tibet. Fly me in twice a week for tea and petit fours. Dearest feminists, we are talking billions.

MARGARET: If I didn't know you were a paranoid schizophrenic, I would think you were a tupperware salesman.

ROSE: *(To Kristen.)* You don't have your price?

KRISTEN: What a yucky thing to say.

ROSE: *(To Margaret.)* You don't have *your* price?

MARGARET: I'm engaged, nutso.

ROSE: Dump him.

MARGARET: Is this a joke, or what?

ROSE: Call it off.

MARGARET: I'm in love.

ROSE: You were in love last year.

MARGARET: That was different.

ROSE: Six times.

MARGARET: Okay, six times.

ROSE: And three weeks ago you went out with somebody else.

MARGARET: For coffee.

ROSE: Right. Coffee. Your first marriage, should it last more than two years, should be put in a natural history museum.

KRISTEN: Easy.

ROSE: You take him.

KRISTEN: I'm afraid I'm not that cynical.

ROSE: Want to end up in Plenty Wood?

KRISTEN: I won't.

ROSE: You don't have a dime, Kristen. Your family doesn't have a dime. You rode the scholarships till they gave out. You're going to end up being a dollar-twenty-five barber.

KRISTEN: It's a little too late in the century to turn into a courtesan.

ROSE: It's a little late in the century to turn into a barber.

KRISTEN: Knock it off.

ROSE: Take him. Get a divorce in two years. Settle for practically nothing, sixty million and the house. Be anything, marry anybody, go anywhere. Don't feed me this romantic, I'm-too-good-for-this, I'm-a-powerful-woman crap. This isn't another antimaterialist, spiritual, self-expanding, liberated bull session. This is millions of dollars cold cash on the barrelhead. I already called him.

MARGARET: Teddy whatsis?

ROSE: Teddy whatsis. Be here in maybe five minutes. You don't have to invent the electric car, cure the cold, find yourself, none of it. It's gonna happen this once and never happen again. It's beyond *Cosmopolitan*. Figure out who you are later. Figure out what you believe later. Sell out and praise the Lord. Don't tell me you're too damn dumb to figure this out.

MARGARET: Could you look at him in the morning?

ROSE: In the morning everybody looks terrible.

KRISTEN: What about him? What about his feelings?

ROSE: He'll love it. He's been waiting for it for years. Come on, look it in the face. When it's over, he'll kiss you good-bye and buy Sharon Stone.

MARGARET: You really are a monster.

ROSE: Don't kid me, ladies. We are born in America. We are middle-class down to our anklets and add-a-beads. We started learning this stuff with our Barbie dolls. And don't give me any "traditional roles" stuff. You think guys wouldn't do this if you had these bucks? And if you don't do it, somebody else will. They will line up from here to Nome, Alaska. And what is your responsibility to yourself? Our responsibility is to our potential. Fifty percent of all American marriages end up in divorce anyway and you know what is given as chief cause? Financial problems. No kidding. And you are doing him a disservice? He's pining away out there. He sits with his back to the cafeteria wall drinking black coffee and wishing he wasn't alone. I mean you aren't hardened cases or something. You can't tell a book by its cover and all that. He's bright. He's a gentleman. Joanie says he practically threw *himself* over the puddles so she wouldn't get wet. I grant you he's short, shy, and myopic, but listen, he is a man among men. What he can do for you, Superman can't do. And, by way of comparison, how hot is anything else we've gotten mixed up with? Your fiancé, Margaret, how many dawns and Bloody Marys have we shared while you agonized? I will, I won't, I will, I can't, I love him, I don't, we don't have the same interests, he's cute. Come on, face it. Prince Charles hasn't showed up. *(There is a knock at the door.)*

MARGARET: *(Mouthing the words and pointing to the door.)* Is that him? *(Rose nods.)*

ROSE: Your carriage waits without. No, no, don't push, don't shove. There's a way to settle this. I've got a quarter. You guys call it. *(There is a knock on the door.)* Bet it or regret it.

KRISTEN: I can't do this. How can I do this?

ROSE: One and only chance. *(Another knock. A pause.)*

KRISTEN: Tails.

MARGARET: Oh, what the hell. Heads. *(Rose flips the coin and holds it out for them to look at as the lights fade.)*

END OF PLAY

Sunday Go to Meetin'
by Shirley Lauro

CHARACTERS

SALLY SUE JONES: Twelve or thirteen. A country girl. Naive but inquisitive. Blond hair, long, tied back at nape of neck with her Sunday bow. Wears Sunday clothes—white or pastel, white high-top shoes. She is a good girl, an old-fashioned girl.

HESTER BLOODWORTH: Fourteen or fifteen. Also a country girl. Hester is the town daredevil. Coquettish and mischievous and always getting into trouble. Also fair-haired. Dressed similarly to Sally Sue.

SARAH WARSAVSKY: Sixteen. Wears babushka on head and long dark skirt, black stockings. She looks very European, Semitic, dark. She has already been through a great deal in her young life and seems much older, much different, and more worldly-wise than the other girls.

Note: Several Yiddish phrases are spoken by Sarah. English translations are included for reference. In production, the actress speaks only the Yiddish words.

Sunday Go to Meetin'

Scene: A rural village in the Midwest. 1905. Sunday morning. Early autumn.

At rise: Lights come up on a country road leading to a Southern Baptist church. A white picket fence lines the road marking off the church property. In the distance we hear the parishioners singing liltingly, slowly:

OFFSTAGE VOICES: *(Singing.)*
"Give me that old-time religion
Give me that old-time religion
Give me that old-time religion
It's good enough for me.
It was good enough for Brother
It was good enough for Sister
It was good enough for Mother
And it's good enough for me—"

> *(Church is about to begin. As their voices drift off, Sally Sue enters on her way to Sunday school. She is twelve or thirteen in her Sunday best: long blond hair held at nape of neck with ribbon, white or pastel dress, white high top shoes, carrying a Bible. As she crosses stage, Hester appears behind her. Hester is a year or so older than Sally Sue and the village daredevil. She is dressed like Sally Sue with her long, fair hair tied at nape of neck with a big bow and carrying her Bible too. Hester has been running to catch up with Sally Sue. She has something important to tell her.)*

HESTER: Psst! Sally? Sally Sue?

SALLY: *(Stops, turns around. She is impressed with Hester and a little afraid of her.)* Yes?

HESTER: *(Giggling, mischievous.)* Wanna go for a little walk with me? Right now??

SALLY: It's Sunday, Hester.

HESTER: (Scoffs.) Well, don't I know it's Sunday!? My Land!

SALLY: Well, I can't go for no walk! I'm almost late right now!

(She starts on her way, Hester trailing her.)

HESTER: (Coaxingly.) Not even for a little bitty ole walk? (She giggles to herself. She has a secret.)

SALLY: (Looking at her, curious.) What kind of walk? I got to go to Sunday school—you do too!

HESTER: (Growing mysterious.) Oh, just a walk down the road, edge a town. Take about fifteen minutes is all—just see the wonders a the Lord all around us to behold—among other things! (She now starts off, leaving Sally in her wake.)

SALLY: (Now runs to catch up.) What other things?

HESTER: (Stops, looking at her; superior.) Oh, things Billy Henderson has told me about.

SALLY: What kinda things he tell you about?

HESTER: (Laughing.) Oh now just look at you! Eyes about to bug out of your head with the curiosity, huh? Wanna come?

SALLY: What things has Billy Henderson told you about? Tell me, and I'll go!

HESTER: Well—you know over to the edge a town—that old warehouse place where the Wilkins lived upstairs and stored their grain downstairs an stuff? That ole spooky ole tumble-down shacky place?

SALLY: What about it?

HESTER: (Very nonchalantly while she drops this.) Well, there's a pack a Jews moved in there—

SALLY: (Astounded.) WHAT??

HESTER: (Still quite casual.) Mmm. Opened up a fruit stand out front Billy says.

SALLY: (Can't believe this.) JEWS??

HESTER: Mmm. Two, three families of 'em—all related—all lookin' jist alike Billy says. See, they bought the place and is movin' in here! PERMANENT!

SALLY: HERE??

HESTER: Mmm. They went right on down to Hawkins Law Office and Real Estate and plunked hundreds and hundreds a dollars down cash! Mr. Hawkins said he couldn't hardly believe his eyes how their menfolks just kept pullin' all this money outta their coat pockets and seams a their coats and jist paid for the whole place right there on the spot!

SALLY: (Bowled over.) No!

HESTER: It's the Lord's truth! See, Billy was jist hangin' around that ole law office and Hawkins came out and told him the whole thing—and then Billy ran on down the road and caught up to 'em and *TALKED* to 'em!

SALLY: Oh Pshaw! What'd they say?

HESTER: Nothin' much Billy could understand—jist talkin' all this foreign jibberty jaw! But Ole Man Hawkins tole Billy they come off a freighter boat from Europe. Landed on the Gulf, then moved on up from New Orleans.

SALLY: Oh my Stars! *LIVE JEWS?!?!* What'd they *look* like? Billy say?

HESTER: Didn't say too much. Funny lookin' though—not nothin' like white folks, now that's a fact.

SALLY: Crime in It'ly! I can't hardly believe it—JEWS!!

HESTER: They're sellin' apples out in front a the place Billy said. Got a wagon full of 'em parked on the road. Windfall.

SALLY: Windfall?

HESTER: Ummm—See, their menfolks took this wagon and went on out to the country—Dabny's farm—and just went right onto his land and picked up the windfall apples outta his orchard, from the ground. And then went on and done the same thing at the Johnson place. And now they're sellin' 'em off, Billy says. Right now. Today.

SALLY: Sunday?

HESTER: Well, they're *heathens*, Sally Sue. Shoot girl! Don't you know nothin'? It don't mean nothing to *them* working on the Lord's Day—hey—you got any money?

SALLY: Jist my Donation is all.

HESTER: Well, I got six cents—wonder how many a them windfall apples that'd buy?

SALLY: I don't know and I don't care! I got to go—
(She starts off, Hester comes after her.)

HESTER: Aw, come on—walk on over there with me—it'd jist take ten minutes—and we could sneak on into church—nobody'll see us or nothin'—Sally Sue? Come on go see—shoot! *(She stands in front of Sally, taking her hand.)*

SALLY: No! I'd just be too scared, Hester! Now let me pass. *(She pushes by Hester who trails her again.)*

HESTER: Don't have to be scared! We don't have to go inside no place or nothin'. Billy says the apples is by the road in front! We could just watch from across the road—hey—we don't even have to buy nothin' if we don't want—jist pass by and stop and take a look—

(She comes in front of Sally again, blocking her way, again Sally pushes her aside.)

HESTER: …and then we'll come right on back to church! Come on!

SALLY: I don't think so, Hester! I got to go to Sunday school, and I jist *know* I'd be too scairt!

HESTER: *(Now flouncing away from Sally in the other direction.)* Well, then I'm goin' on by myself—and you ain't never gonna git no chance to see any live Jews or nothin' ever again—not with *me* you ain't! An I'm gonna tell Billy what an ole sissy scaredy-cat you are! *(She is almost off, then coquettishly she turns back.)* Oh my!—I did remember one other thing Billy had said—

SALLY: *(Almost off in other direction, but her curiosity is too great. She stops, turns.)* What?

HESTER: *(Coming back toward her, giggling.)* The Jew men got theirselves horns on their heads!

(She laughs out loud now and Sally starts giggling too, imagining this. Hester now pursues this.)

HESTER: And know what *else?*

SALLY: *(Still giggling, succumbs.)* What?

HESTER: They wears *hats* all day long and *never* takes 'em off—jist to hide them horns!

(This sends them both into more fits of laughter.)

SALLY: No! I never heard such a thing in my life!

HESTER: And know what *else?*

SALLY: What?

HESTER: They got *tails!*

(She laughs more and Sally does too.)

SALLY: TAILS??? Oh, Lawd! TAILS??

HESTER: Billy says—*(She is convulsed.)*—Billy—Billy says—they wears long *coats* to cover *them* up—

SALLY: Land a Goshen, Hester! *(She is laughing hysterically.)* Land!

HESTER: Hey—come on—come an go! You know you're jist *dyin'* to see it all! You jist *know* you are! Come on!!! *(And she takes her hand pulling her in the direction of the edge of town.)*

SALLY: Oh, Hester—Oh, Hester, I shouldn't—I jist shouldn't go at all—*(But she is allowing herself to be pulled.)* Well, we can't stay long—we got to git right back fast, hear??? Promise me that!

HESTER: *(As they both exit, running.)* Sure, sure! Now come on—come on— Ooooeee!!!

(As lights fade we hear the girls singing as they run along the country road; it is a popular song from long ago.)

SALLY AND HESTER: *(Offstage.)*

"Oh, we belong to Uncle Sam,
Sing-song Kitsy Kitsy Kai-me-oh.
Oh, we belong to Uncle Sam,
Sing-song Kitsy Kitsy Kai-me-oh.
Kay-mo, Kai-mo, dear old Dad,
M'hey, M'hi, M'hum-drum
I go way, we go way, they go way
Uruguay, Paraguay,
Oh! We belong to Uncle Sam!
Sing-song Kitsy Kitsy Kai-me-oh!"

(Their voices fade as we come up on another part of the road which runs diagonally. There is a wagon filled with apples on one side of it and some bushes on the other. Hester and Sally's voices die out as they come onstage, and spying the apple wagon, stop, hiding themselves behind the bush, warily looking out, whispering.)

HESTER: There it is—now all we gotta do is wait—here—stay here—and be quiet and wait—

SALLY: *(Rapidly losing her courage.)* Oh, I jist feel so funny Hester! I truly do! I don't know what it's gonna be like seein' no Jews. But it *sure* feels evil! It bein' Sunday and all! It jist feels EVIL—oh, HESTER—

(Sarah now enters, carrying a sign, laboriously handmade and handwritten that says: "APPLES 5¢." She is the oldest daughter of the family. She is a teenager also. Wears a babushka on her head and a long dark skirt and black stockings. She looks very European, Semitic. She now sticks the sign on the wagon and rearranges the fruit a little. The girls are whispering.)

SALLY: Oh, Land! Look at her with that ole funny scarf and all—and so dark! She looks evil Hester! Jist so evil!

HESTER: *(Intrigued.)* Hey—know what they say?

SALLY: *(Wishing she hadn't come.)* What?

HESTER: All their women opens up sideways down there—

SALLY: *(Shocked.)* What?

HESTER: Chink women does too—slanty like their eyes! *(She giggles.)* Jist like a cat.

SALLY: Stop that! Don't you go talkin' filthy dirty like that on the Lord's day!

Oh, Hester don't! We're gonna git punished for sure—lightnin' or thunder or tornadoes or—

HESTER: Oh hush up, scaredy-cat! Ain't nothin gonna happen to us—

SALLY: Well don't you talk dirty like that again!

HESTER: *(Giggling.)* Ain't dirty—it's a fact a life!

(Sarah turns and now exits.)

HESTER: Hey—know what else is a fact a life?

SALLY: No—and I don't wanna! I jist want outta here!

HESTER: Their men is in two parts down there—

SALLY: Huh?

HESTER: They cut 'em in half down there when they's babies. They got two dinghies!

SALLY: *(Stunned.)* Oh Land and they livin' HERE!? PLEASE!!! LET'S GO!!

(She grabs her hand, tries to pull her away.)

HESTER: NO! Let go! I wanna see her some more—besides she's jist a girl. She can't hurt us—but you better not bring your brother round here 'cause they kill other people's baby *boys*. Now that's a fact a—

(Sarah now reappears carrying a stack of baskets for her apples. She hears and sees Sally and Hester.)

SARAH: *(Speaks hesitantly, with a heavy accent. These are memorized phrases she doesn't understand.)* Hello—Hello—How—are—you—? *(She starts to cross the road, trying to see them behind the tree, shading her eyes. Now she points back to wagon. These words she understands.)* Apples? Five cents?— Du vielst? (Trans: Do you want?)*

SALLY: *(Terrified now.)* Oh Law! She's talking jibberty jaw! She's puttin' some kinda curse on us, Hester! Oh, Law!

HESTER: *(Now takes a stand against Sarah, stepping out into the road.)* No! Don't you come no step closer to us! We don't want nothing off you! We don't want no stolen apples!

SARAH: *(Not comprehending at all.)* "Stolen?" Ich forshtayin zee nisht! *(Trans: I don't understand you!)* (Again she points to her apples.)* Apples? Five cents?

SALLY: Oh law! She cursed us again! On my Stars! Let's run! She's a *witch!*

HESTER: *(Refusing to be intimidated.)* No! I said no! We don't want your stolen apples! And you keep off a us! This here's a public road and you keep away, you hear. Or I'll git my Pa! You got no business here! That's stolen goods!

SARAH: *(Smiling, holding out basket.)* Hello—how—are—you—*(Her smile fades. She sees something is very wrong.)* Vos iss de mer—vos iss de mer mitt ouns? *(Trans: What is the matter—what is the matter with you?)*

(At the Yiddish, Hester, terrified, grabs stone, hurls it, hitting Sarah on the arm. Her baskets fall to the ground, and Sarah cries out in pain. At this Sally breaks away and starts running off, screaming.)

SALLY: WITCH! WITCH!!

HESTER: Now you keep away from us! Don't you put no curse on us. JIST KEEP AWAY!! JIST KEEP AWAY!! *(She is backing up, holding Sarah at bay, then runs off.)*

SARAH: *(She stands, sobbing, holding her arm. After a beat, with bitter anger, she screams after them.)* SHIKSAS!!! SHIKSAS!!! *(Trans: Gentile girls! Gentile girls!) (After a moment she wipes her eyes, picks up her pile of baskets and goes to the wagon, stacking them on the ground. Then, determinedly, she takes her sign and sticks it in the front row of apples so it will be more visible. Then she turns and looks down the road in the direction of the girls. After a moment, she yanks her babushka from her head and twists it quickly into a long cord. She now gathers her long dark hair at the nape of her neck and ties it with the cord in the manner of Sally and Hester. She now looks down the road the other way for her next customers; with as much bravado as she can muster, hiding her fear, she begins reciting.)* "Hello? How are you? Apples, five cents. Hello? How are you—"*

(In the distance we hear Sally and Hester singing as they run along the country road to church.)

SALLY AND HESTER: *(Offstage.)*

"Oh, we belong to Uncle Sam,
Sing-song Kitsy Kitsy kai-me-oh.
We belong to Uncle Sam—
(Their voices grow fainter and fainter as we go to black.)

END OF PLAY

Broken Hearts
by Kevin R. McLeod

CHARACTERS
DIANNE

MARGARET

GRANDMA

Broken Hearts

Dark. The sound of a heart monitor. The blip goes flat. Sound fades out. Lights slowly fade up as a pool of light to reveal Dianne lying on her back on the floor. She is perfectly still. All at once she jerks awake as if waking from one of those awful falling dreams. She slowly looks about. She begins to move and run her hands over herself. The remainder of the stage has slowly faded up. There is a door. Margaret sits in a very plain chair crocheting. Around her are many afghans.

MARGARET: Oh, good, company…
> *(Dianne continues to run her hands over her legs, then the floor. She looks about, confused.)*

MARGARET: Kind of disorienting, isn't it?

DIANNE: What happened? Where am I?
> *(Margaret laughs.)*

DIANNE: I feel so GOOD—like I'm floating—*(Directly.)* Where am I?

MARGARET: Look down, dear.

DIANNE: *(Horror.)* Oh, no. No. This can't—

MARGARET: It can—

DIANNE: They must be having problems—

MARGARET: I'll say!

DIANNE: They explained this might happen… I had such hopes… *(Sits on floor.)* …it's not fair…

MARGARET: I said the same thing.

DIANNE: That's the end of that. I'm dead, aren't I?

MARGARET: Not exactly… *(Stops crocheting.)* That down there is consciousness, this is UNconsciousness, and through that door over there is *(Big voice.)* THE GREAT BEYOND. *(Resumes crocheting.)* Right now you're unconscious.

DIANNE: But I feel so good. I haven't felt this good for years—

MARGARET: You've been restored. You're as you were at your peak. And I must say, you peaked awfully young.

DIANNE: I'm only eighteen—

MARGARET: You poor thing. And I thought it was bad when I cashed it in at forty-three.

DIANNE: I've been sick for a long time—

MARGARET: When was the last time you felt really good—

DIANNE: I guess my thirteenth birthday. Running around with my cousins. We played baseball, I hit a home run and won the game.

MARGARET: Then you're thirteen now. Myself, well, I guess I'm twenty-four, just after my first baby, Paulie Jr., was born.

DIANNE: You're "unconscious" too?

MARGARET: *(Laughs.)* Heavens no! I'm dead! They're going to plant me in the ground tomorrow. I'm just hanging around here to keep an eye on my "survived by's."

DIANNE: Then, you've already gone through—*(Gestures toward door.)*

MARGARET: Oh, yes, two weeks ago—

DIANNE: I guess I should—*(Starts toward door.)*

MARGARET: I wouldn't if I were you. That's what I did. Barrelled through on my own. Took matters into my own hands. *(Stops crocheting.)* Let me tell you, it is worse than the DMV through that tunnel. Tests to take. You wait all day in line, but it's the wrong line!—Only to find I wasn't even supposed to be there yet. All the while my body lays in a coma for two weeks. I tried to go back down, but I was pretty far gone… Poor Paul, he so hoped I'd come to. *(Resumes crocheting.)* It would have been much less frustrating had I just waited for my guide to come for me…

DIANNE: Guide? There's a guide?

MARGARET: Who was the last person really close to you to die?

DIANNE: My grandma, I guess… Two, three years ago—

MARGARET: Then she'll be your guide. My nana was my guide too—Whisked me through orientation in no time flat. She even FINALLY taught me how to crochet. I could never get the hang of it, and now I can't stop—

DIANNE: *(Laughs.)* I hardly think Grandma is capable of guiding anyone. She died completely off her beam… She had this fondness for her cordless beater—Took it everywhere. She'd sit on her porch swing and rev it up at passing cars. Serve her coffee, and she'd whip it to a froth. It seems so funny now… She was the only one who could talk to me without crying when we found out. Then all of a sudden she went weird… I was so mad at her for that…

MARGARET: You'll be surprised. She is restored…

DIANNE: *(Looking down.)* Oh, my God!!!

MARGARET: *(Looks in that direction.)* So much blood! Honey, what are they doing to you?

DIANNE: It's a heart transplant… The old one was never very good. Then after thirteen it started to shut down. It doesn't seem to be going too smoothly, does it? Darn, I waited so long for this—

MARGARET: Look over here—down there—see that man sitting in the pew? That's my Paul. Just a short while ago he agreed to let the doctors harvest what organs they could—I believe you've got my heart!

DIANNE: But it's spewing all over the place… I'm sorry—

MARGARET: Hey, kid, it's not your fault. Human error strikes again—damn good heart. No smoking, saturated fats, or caffeine. Plenty of raw vegetables. Airdyne every morning. Jane Fonda Step Aerobics Monday, Wednesday, and Friday. Mallwalkers Tuesday, Thursday, Saturday. A brisk hike every Sunday afternoon. But one quick flick of a knife and you're shooting off like a geyser. It's a healthy heart—physically. Emotionally, well, that's all in the head, isn't it?

DIANNE: So quick this happens. It's over—

MARGARET: It ain't over till it's over, sweetie. *(Resumes crocheting.)* Be thankful you're not down there right now, it looks pretty painful—

DIANNE: It sure does…

MARGARET: Don't look anymore, you'll just be upset.

DIANNE: Yeah, you're right… *(Turns away.)* what to do—

MARGARET: Would you like an afghan? I've got plenty.

DIANNE: No, no I'm fine…

MARGARET: Unconscious, dear… You're not dead yet…

DIANNE: You'd think there'd at least be magazines or something—

MARGARET: *(Laughs.)* Just like at the doctor's office—everyone takes them back to the examination rooms—

DIANNE: Please, don't start on doctors' offices—

MARGARET: Well, someone should be bringing back a stack of *Highlights for Children* pretty soon—

DIANNE: I've read every issue since I was thirteen… *(Walks around, bored.)* …I hate waiting…

MARGARET: I was like that too…

DIANNE: How did you, you know—

MARGARET: Check out of the Hotel California!

DIANNE: Yes! Yes!

MARGARET: *(Suddenly very serious.)* Not enough fat in my arteries…

DIANNE: *(Incredulous.)* What?

MARGARET: No, not enough fat in my arteries... My blood just whisked through so fast I overheated like a radiator— *(Starts to laugh.)*

DIANNE: *(Laughing.)* You're kidding—

MARGARET: Yes, I'm kidding... Vanity killed me...self-indulgence killed me... I killed my self...

DIANNE: *(Suddenly this has become serious.)* Oh, suicide—

MARGARET: *(Laughs.)* Honey, I was too into myself to do that... Look, it's a long story...

DIANNE: I don't have much else to do...

MARGARET: After twenty-plus years, Paul and I had a huge house, a small mortgage and three sons who were turning into fine young men—

DIANNE: Sounds perfect—

MARGARET: Perfectly boring. Paul and I still loved each other, we just weren't "in love" anymore. I found out Paul was seeing a younger woman. I went crazy! Someone had to be blamed, so I blamed myself—I wasn't young enough, pretty enough, smart enough, good enough, I wasn't "enough." I shifted it into overdrive. I became Superwoman, earth mother, Donna Reed, you name it—all rolled into one...

DIANNE: But was it enough?

MARGARET: He fell in love with her! What did he want? Youth. You know how gravity starts to tear at you once you hit forty—oh, of course not, you're only eighteen. Well, let me tell you, it's no picnic. Your whole body starts to fall apart—*(Realizes.)* Oh, I'm sorry—

DIANNE: Hey, it's okay... So you went to a plastic surgeon, right?

MARGARET: You know this story?

DIANNE: I have a lot of time to watch soap operas—

MARGARET: I didn't just go to the plastic surgeon, I was a regular. No sooner was the swelling gone, than the swelling was back. I was nipped, tucked, lifted, sucked off, and added to! I LOVED IT!! I LOVED ME!! Pretty soon Paul didn't matter, all I had left was this shell to work on...shell... I couldn't even recognize my own reflection...

DIANNE: So, you really did "kill" your "self"...

MARGARET: Yes, I guess I did... The irony is I wrapped the Benz around a telephone pole on my way to have another facelift. BAM through that windshield, and there wasn't a face left to lift!

DIANNE: Is that her down there with him?

MARGARET: *(Small laugh.)* So it is! Good, he needs someone to hold him right now. He never left while I was in the coma. He really did love me. I just wish there was a way to tell him I understand, that it's okay. He loves her. He needs to hold her tight and never let go—

DIANNE: —We both died with broken hearts…

MARGARET: Dianna May, what a pessimist you are—

DIANNE: You know my name?

MARGARET: *(Smiles.)* Of course. And I know that your bleeding has stopped!

DIANNE: *(Looks down.)* No! It has—

MARGARET: Maybe it's time to go back down—

DIANNE: *(Sharp.)* No! No, if it's okay, I'd rather stay here… I've gotten very comfortable…

MARGARET: Look, you mustn't get comfortable here. You are not meant to stay here. That's why there is no place to sit, no magazines to read. You must *want* to go back… This is nothingness, down there is life… You've got a second chance. Don't waste it here in nothing.

DIANNE: It all looks so painful down there—

MARGARET: It frequently is…

DIANNE: *(Crouches on the floor, almost fetal.)* When I was twelve, all I wanted to be was a teacher. I loved school. When I was thirteen I blacked out playing tetherball and never went back to regular school again… I came to in ICU with what seemed like a million tubes down my throat and in my arm. Machines hissed. Doctors shook their heads. Mom and Dad cried a whole bunch… Grandma was the one who told me what was going on. I was very sick. I cried and she rocked me in her arms and told me she wouldn't let anything hurt me. And I believed her… But I didn't get better, and Grandma got funny and died, and Mom and Dad cried a lot more… *(Starts to cry herself.)*

MARGARET: *(Back to her crocheting, sighs.)* Kind of disorienting, isn't it ?
(During the above, the door has slowly swung open. All at once bright light spills from the open doorway. Grandma steps through. She is dressed simply. She looks to be in her twenties.)

GRANDMA: Dianna May? I thought you were in here!

DIANNE: Grandma?

GRANDMA: *(Reveals cordless mixer. Revs it.)* How'd you guess?
(They hug.)

GRANDMA: So, kiddo, looking very good! Good enough to eat all gone. *(Hugs her again.)* How I've missed my little girl—You're not still pissed I died, are you?

DIANNE: Grandma, you look so, so—

GRANDMA: I know, ain't it a hoot? I got my old body, my brain back, and I got to keep the beater to boot!

DIANNE: *(Stops and looks at her.)* Grandma, I, I—*(Margaret clears her throat.)* Oh, I'd like you to meet—

GRANDMA: Oh, hi there, Margaret—

MARGARET: Helen, so glad you came. Dianne here was about to set up camp.

GRANDMA: What's the matter, kid? I thought you were getting a new ticker—Margaret's in fact! Healthy as a horse I hear!!

DIANNE: It hasn't gone very well. Look—

GRANDMA: Ooh, my. Quite a little mishap there.

DIANNE: Grandma, I don't want to go back to that. I'm tired of always being sick… Mom and Dad's faces every time I go back to the hospital.
(Starts to cry. Grandma hugs her and rocks her.)

DIANNE: Hoping maybe this time I'll get better, but knowing I really never will—

GRANDMA: There, there, pumpkin. It's okay. Grandma's not gonna let anything hurt you—

DIANNE: Take me through the doorway, Grandma, so I can be with you—
(Starts to lead Grandma towards door.)

GRANDMA: Ah, ah, ah—not so fast, honey… I can't take you through, not yet—

DIANNE: But—

GRANDMA: There are a few things you have to do.

DIANNE: What?

GRANDMA: First you have to get through this operation. Then there's a teachers' college you have to go to, and a school you have to teach in. It will take a little longer than you want, but you'll just have to be patient for once. Somewhere out there is a handsome young man who wants to take you to dinner, then eventually he'll marry you. Then there are a few million other things you have to do, and *then* you will come here out of a peaceful sleep. *(Starts toward door.)* Then I will take you through. *(She steps through the door. It swings shut. The bright light is gone.)*

DIANNE: I love you, Grandma—

GRANDMA: See you later, alligator—
(Dianne looks at the door, stares down at the operating room. The surrounding light begins to fade. Dianne is in her original pool of light. She takes a

deep breath and lies down on the floor. Margaret looks up from her crocheting just as her light fades away.)

MARGARET: Dianna May—when you get out of the hospital, look up Paul Gower in Flagstaff, Arizona. Tell him Margaret understands, and that he deserves to be happy— *(Light out.)*
(Dianne's light goes out fast. Darkness. Sound of a heart monitor.)

END OF PLAY

Body Talk
by Tanya Palmer

CHARACTERS

1

2

3

Body Talk

Images of women's bodies—Female iconography. Then flesh. Maps projected onto flesh. Then bodies disappear. Lights up on three women, isolated from one another. The first woman is captured, like in a photograph.

1. Exaltation

I see myself in a drugstore window. Tall. Wearing big boots that make me feel like I'm strutting everywhere I go. Supercool. Tight pants. Black. And I can't believe it's me 'cause I'm beautiful. I don't even recognize myself, it's like a whole other individual has taken over my reflection. She's thin and she's got a big smile and she stands with her shoulders back, not crouching forward, and she looks mean through her happiness. Tough. And I love her. Love her. ME. I recognize that stupid shy scared sadness not quite ready to leave her face. And I hear her fear. What do you do when you've never liked yourself, never known how to. Always thought you were nothing good, only something to hide. But one day like magic you see yourself full of love for yourself like a spell has been cast. I see, touch, taste that face. My face. And my body and my beauty shines a beam of light so bright I'm propelled forward, down the street and into a coffee shop. I enter with my big thick boots and flash a big beautiful smile at the girl behind the counter with the cat eyes and the golden hair. She's wearing a shirt that is sea foam, that's the color—sea foam. "I love your shirt." She smiles and says "thanks" and I'm feeling so sexy, like heat just at the surface of every part of me, she can feel it too. We exchange glances like it's too bad we're in a crowded coffee shop otherwise we could rip out clothes off, except my boots, and see just how fucking amazing we are. Everyone looks up and takes me in. I smile a huge, generous, I'm-giving-you-a-piece-of-me smile to this man with graying hair sitting on a black and pink stool and he smiles back. We are radiant, the two of us together, and me and the cat-eyed girl are radiant too. I turn again and flash my smile to the whole fucking place and they smile back and I think this, Thomas Merton, is an example of universal love. This is me saying I love myself so much I can love every single one of you, that's how much love I've got in me. I buy a mochaccino 'cause it's the most expensive drink, and I love sugar and I eat pastry 'cause why the fuck not and I love this and myself and I don't need anyone else to tell me why.

2. (Diving, Drowning, Driving)

I don't know my body too well 'cause I never felt like it really belonged to me. I only floated around in it like it was a canoe, traveling with me as a passenger inside. Except I had no paddles. No control. No knowledge of how a canoe operates. How do you steer a canoe? What is a canoe made of? I didn't know it. Or know how to know it. And when you first touched me and I kissed you back and we ended up in my bed and your thin body and your tiny hips scooped me up into the center of you and traveled into the center of me and I felt comfortable and happy and I thought this is my home. Right here, that point where my body meets your body that's the place I can be I, if you see what I'm trying to say. You were hesitant, which made it even better. I tricked you into my body— that guest house I'd been crashing in for a long time, but now I'm home and I can relax and unpack. You welcome me in, your tiny hips, your curving stomach, your thin chest. I hold you against that flesh around me like a child and you crawl down and rest your head on my belly and I cry, just a little so you might not notice, 'cause you are so beautiful. Most of all this is so beautiful, this flesh house of connected bodies where I live and see myself for the first time. But it's disappearing. I know that. I pretend not to, but I do know. That day when we went out driving in the car, my car, I'm driving, you're holding a map, it's open on your lap and you're saying nothing. Nothing. I can't breathe in the silence. We're driving through the prairies and there's nothing around but farmers' fields and highways and I don't know where we're going or why, so I keep trying to think of anything to say, like "There's Black Diamond, that's where they make that cheese," or "What do you think they're growing in that field, do you think that's canola? My father used to call canola rapeseed. I hated hearing those words coming out of his mouth." And I keep talking, and you smile at me, and sometimes you speak, but it's still silence 'cause it's not speaking to me, could be to anyone. Suddenly I know each moment we spend in silence our bodies are stepping further and further away. I can feel myself disappear. *(Lights begin to fade out.)* Your thin hips, your beautiful child's body are floating away and I try to crawl back into my canoe, but it's not there anymore, I've given it away. I look in the mirror to remind myself what I look like, but I don't recognize myself as me. What is what I like and what is what we like, do you know what I mean? Do I like going to movies, or do we? Do I like sleeping till noon, or do we? Do I like making hash browns for breakfast and eat them sitting outside on the step and do I like strong coffee and do I like the clothes I'm wearing and do I like my new haircut, or do We? Where do I go to feel at home now? Where did I go? Where am I? Is any of this making any sense?

3.

I'm trying. To be positive. If I don't I start having panic attacks. Don't look alarmed. Well, I guess it is alarming. It's alarming for me too. When suddenly I start to breathe really quickly and shallow. Hyperventilating. I don't always know what starts it off, it's usually nothing concrete, it's something in my head, a thought like for example "that was the stupidest fucking thing you could have said." "Idiot FAT UGLY idiot." And from that point on I lose a sense of connection to real events. "You're stupid, you can't do anything you'll never do anything, ever. Ever. Ever." And why not? It doesn't make sense. I'm smart. I'm … I'm what? I'm not a fucking thing. I'm a vacuous vacuum. I'm a collection of sour gases. I'm a series of mistakes. That's when I start to hyperventilate. So I'll be positive, so I don't have to put you through that. So as not to alarm you. When I was growing up I went to the Unitarian church and they taught us this chant: I am lovable and capable. So as to empower the soul. If you love yourself, then you can love others. So the theory goes. So I say that to myself. I am lovable and capable. Or I change the order. I am capable and lovable. Or I say one without the other. I am capable. But am I lovable? And I look down at my body and it's been destroyed by my mind. The sour gases turn my skin sour. It's not smooth, it's scaly, it's not tight, it bursts into hideous bubbles of white fat. FAT. I want to punish this fucking skin for being so fucking ugly it makes me sick so I try different things, like sometimes I hit my head against the wall over and over again until I almost pass out. Or I punch myself in the gut or I just stare at my face and scrub at it so maybe it'll disappear. My body is covered in a cloak that says to people, stay away, 'cause if you get too close I'll contaminate you with my sour gases. But then I'm lonely so I say to that face in words that slice through flesh, "You're incapable incapable incapable of making friends. No one could ever love you. You're unlovable because you're nothing but badness." So if you want to know why I'm hyperventilating it's 'cause if I didn't force myself to breathe I'd stop. My body is making one last effort to bring my mind back to life. All I can do is cry or scream 'cause that's how much I hate me. The sour juices stewing and simmering inside. Whisper to my flesh. You have committed a terrible sin. How do I atone?

1. Escape

So I get in my truck and it's a stick shift which is so I'm in control and I'm going and I get on the road. And the black and green and beautiful yellow of the prairies is flying by me and I'm screaming inside my body "I'm leaving I'm leaving I'm leaving my home!" I let my truck say goodbye to the land that raised me. 'Cause I can't say it myself, not out loud. Suddenly my body and my truck are the same animal, both driving through the rain, skin flying past the canola fields, tires driving over asphalt. Going FAST. Claresholm where we'd always stop at the 7-Eleven for Slurpees, Fort Macleod where they roast the turkeys in a big metal torture chamber. See you NEVER. I don't want to stop, ever ever. Only to piss or shit or pump gas. I feel ecstasy. My boots pump hard against the gas pedal, my hand grips the stick.

3. I lift this hand from the steering wheel for a moment and reach out the window, searching for the passing air. On the highway, the wind rushes beside my head, ear. Hand, fingers unfolding. My hand is out the window, my arm is riding the wind, floating, up and down, waving—like waves on the ocean.

2. Landscapes are moving past me like slides or cue cards, changing faster and faster. Mountains, lakes, pastures,

Driving through Colorado, New Mexico.

Now I'm in canyon, red rock surrounding me, above me.

3. sssslipping…

1. Sexy place that canyon.

2. Leaving Flatland. Fatherland. Homeland.

1. I run through ripples in the rock, feeling them beneath my skin. Rocks all around and ruins. It starts to get dark, so I stop below a canyon and put up my tent, surrounded by couples wearing hip outdoor wear and driving Jeeps. A van pulls up and three women pour out. They are wearing dresses, loose, dropping to the ground. One chain-smokes. The other listens. And the third, the tallest, watches and sees. She is the most beautiful and clearly the leader. They move around her cautiously. Gathering their gear from

the back of the van, laughing, they brush against one another, looking for excuses to touch. They set up in the center of the campground, surrounded by rising red rock. As the light of the sun vanishes completely, the light of their fire rises up and with it is the sound of their voices, these three women singing. Chanting. Bellowing. My friend whispers to me,

3. "They're witches."

1. Suddenly their sound takes flight. Shooting up into a beam of light, my sight paralysed by one image—the flame and the woman, tall and beautiful, her silhouette projected onto the canyon wall, the flame licking her shadow. My body, caught in the upward motion, floats between the canyon walls and the earth. Feet, thighs, cunt, belly, flesh, tits, neck, collarbones, cheeks, eyes, hair, swept up, floating in the fragrance of their chant. My body is a part of the air, the canyon, the earth. Flesh is no longer simply flesh, it is an element that creates the earth. It takes on divinity.

The next morning the women are talking and eating, one is smoking, they laugh. But quietly. Compactly. Nothing remarkable. When I get into my truck and drive away, I carry with me my roots which travel above, below and through the earth and air which carry me. I. Feel. At home. Inside. My body. Everywhere I go.

END OF PLAY

Plays
for
Two Men and One Woman

Lynette Has Beautiful Skin
by Jane Anderson

CHARACTERS

LYNETTE

BOBBY

LARRY

TIME AND PLACE

The present.

A pizza parlor.

N.B. [/ means the next line of dialogue begins here.]

Lynette Has Beautiful Skin

Frank's Pizza. Larry, Bobby, and Lynette are hanging out. Bobby and Lynette are sitting on one side of the booth, very close. Bobby is picking at Lynette's pizza.

LARRY: Her name is Judy…

LYNETTE: Huh?

LARRY: Judy.

LYNETTE: Bobby, c'mon. Leave me something.

BOBBY: I'm just tasting.

LYNETTE: Look, you're picking it all apart. It's unappetizing.

BOBBY: I just wanna see if it's good enough for you.

LYNETTE: Larry, make him stop.

LARRY: *(Automatically.)* Bobby stop.

BOBBY: C'mon, don't ya wanna share with me?

LYNETTE: Eat your own.

BOBBY: I wanna eat yours. Don't you wanna eat mine?

LYNETTE: *(Laughing.)* God, you're a pig. Larry, tell him to stop.

LARRY: Bobby, stop.

BOBBY: *(To Larry, re: Lynette.)* Jesus, doesn't she have great skin?

LYNETTE: Cut it out, Bobby.

BOBBY: She has outstanding skin, doesn't she?

LYNETTE: *(Laughing.)* Shut up!

BOBBY: Hey, don't interrupt me when I'm talking about you. I happen to think you have very delicious skin.

LYNETTE: Larry, tell him to stop.

LARRY: Stop.

BOBBY: *(Whispering to Larry.)* Fantastic skin.

LYNETTE: *(To Larry.)* Tell him to stop.

LARRY: Stop.

(A beat.)

LARRY: *(Trying to get back to a conversation.)* So anyway…

BOBBY: So, you were saying?

LYNETTE: Yeah, the girl, you're seeing a girl?

LARRY: Yeah…

(Bobby takes a bite of Lynette's pizza. She smacks his hand.)

LYNETTE: Bobby, get outta there!/ I can't believe you.

BOBBY: You were saying, Larry, what?

LARRY: This girl…

LYNETTE: Dammit, Bobby.

BOBBY: *(To Lynette, re: pizza.)* I'll buy you another. You want another?

LYNETTE: No, I want to eat the slice I have now. You always do this to me.

BOBBY: What? What am I always doing to you?

LYNETTE: You're always eating my food.

BOBBY: When?

LYNETTE: Like now. Like all the time.

BOBBY: *(To Larry, amused.)* I do?

LYNETTE: All the time.

BOBBY: Your food tastes better.

LYNETTE: It really bothers me, Bobby.

BOBBY: OK. I won't do it anymore.

LYNETTE: OK.

BOBBY: OK.

(They kiss. A beat.)

LARRY: I'm gonna go.

BOBBY: Where're you/going?

LYNETTE: Where're you going, Larry?

LARRY: I don't know. I thought I'd go.

BOBBY: Stay.

LYNETTE: Yeah, Larry, stay.

LARRY: I dunno …

BOBBY: C'mon, I'll buy you another slice. You want another slice?

LARRY: I'm not that hungry for another one.

BOBBY: Then hang out.

LYNETTE: Yeah, Larry, hang out.

BOBBY: How's your car?

LARRY: My car?

BOBBY: Yeah, you get the distributor fixed?

LARRY: I had to replace it.

BOBBY: That's a son of a bitch. Where'd you go?

LARRY: Brandt's.

BOBBY: Brandt's is overpriced. You shoulda gone to Conway's.

LARRY: I went to Conway's. They were out of stock.

BOBBY: Depends who you ask. You talk to Frank?

LARRY: No.

BOBBY: You should of talked to Frank. He can get you anything. At half the price. Brandt's, you pay too much.

(Lynette is playing with her straw, bored. Bobby puts his arm around her.)

BOBBY: So what are you doing?

LYNETTE: Nothing.

BOBBY: Nothing? What are you doing with the straw?

LYNETTE: Nothing.

(Bobby grabs the straw and puts it down Lynette's blouse. Lynette squeals.)

LYNETTE: Bobby, what're you doing?

BOBBY: Nothing.

LYNETTE: Larry, tell him to stop.

LARRY: Stop. *(Larry looks like he wants to go.)*

BOBBY: *(To Larry.)* You want another Coke? Let me get you a Coke. *(Getting up.)* I'll get you another Coke. *(To Lynette.)* You want another Diet?

LYNETTE: Yeah, a Diet.

(Bobby moves off to the counter.)

LYNETTE: So how's your job?

LARRY: It's OK.

LYNETTE: Who's that girl, wasn't there a girl?

LARRY: Yeah, I was saying… Judy.

LYNETTE: You still seeing her?

LARRY: It's hot and cold.

LYNETTE: That's OK, that's OK. I was hot and cold with Bobby. It's part of the game.

LARRY: I can't tell with her.

LYNETTE: I played very cold. But I'd give him signals. She give you signals?

LARRY: I dunno. She gives me looks.

LYNETTE: That's good, that's good. Looks are good.

LARRY: I've seen her looking at me, but it's hard to tell.

LYNETTE: Beginnings are hard, they're very hard. My beginning with Bobby was very complex.

LARRY: Uh-huh.

LYNETTE: He was deeply troubled. His family. You ever meet his family?

LARRY: Yeah.

LYNETTE: So you know.

LARRY: Yeah, I've met them once or twice.

LYNETTE: You can't just walk right into Bobby's life. You have to give him lots of room. Even now.

LARRY: Yeah.

LYNETTE: He needs his independence but he wants to be close.

LARRY: Yeah, I think Judy might be/like that...

LYNETTE: It's hard, it's hard sometimes. Bobby is a very complicated man.

LARRY: Uh-huh.

LYNETTE: To Bobby intimacy means control. He wants his independence but he wants to control. But to me, intimacy means trust. I'm very into trust and Bobby's into control. You know what I mean?

LARRY: Yeah, I like to trust...

LYNETTE: That's very rare. Most men are controllers and most women are trusters.

LARRY: Yeah?

LYNETTE: Oh sure, men trusters are very special, very rare.

LARRY: Well, you know, I'm not a truster all the time.

LYNETTE: That's OK, that's OK. You can't be. Or else you'd be a victim.

LARRY: No, I don't consider myself a victim. Neither are you.

LYNETTE: No, you're right.

LARRY: So how long it take you guys to go to bed?

LYNETTE: First date.

LARRY: You had that kind of attraction, you wanted to do it that soon?

LYNETTE: Sure.

LARRY: And it was good?

LYNETTE: Incredible.

LARRY: Was it love? Were you in love?

LYNETTE: It was an attraction.

LARRY: How long it take you to fall in love?

LYNETTE: It was a while. I fell in love first but I didn't tell Bobby so he wouldn't freak out.

LARRY: So how long you been together?

LYNETTE: Since we fucked, five years. We've only been in love for four. Actually four for me, three and a half for Bobby.

LARRY: So do you think Judy is playing it cool so she doesn't scare me off?

LYNETTE: Maybe.

LARRY: But she doesn't have to with me.

LYNETTE: You're a very special man, Larry.

LARRY: Well…

LYNETTE: Believe it.

(*A beat. Bobby comes back with the drinks.*)

BOBBY: So Larry, how's work?

LARRY: It's OK. I was/telling Lynette…

(*Bobby puts a piece of ice down Lynette's blouse.*)

LYNETTE: Shit, Bobby! Whatta ya doing!!

(*Bobby holds Lynette's arms so she can't get the ice out.*)

BOBBY: So what were you saying, Larry?

LARRY: Yeah, I was saying, you know,/work is OK…

LYNETTE: (*Laughing and screaming.*) Bobby, let go! It's cold! Let go!

BOBBY: How's that girl you're seeing,/ what's her name, Judy?

LYNETTE: I got ice between my tits! Larry tell him/ to let go!

BOBBY: Judy, that her name?

LARRY: Judy, yeah.

LYNETTE: Larry, tell him to let go!

BOBBY: (*To Lynette.*) Where is it? (*Reaching in her blouse.*) Lemme get it. Lemme get it for you.

LYNETTE: Larry, tell him to stop.

LARRY: (*Getting bored.*) Stop.

LYNETTE: Bobby, Larry told you to stop.

BOBBY: OK, OK, I'll stop.

(*Bobby lets go of her. Lynette looks down her blouse for the ice.*)

LYNETTE: There's a wet spot. It left a wet spot all over my blouse.

BOBBY: Here, take a napkin.

LYNETTE: Jesus, Bobby.

BOBBY: You loved it.

LYNETTE: No I didn't. It was stupid.

BOBBY: You were laughing. (*To Larry.*) Didn't you hear her laughing?

(*A beat.*)

LARRY: What time is it?

BOBBY: Around two.

LARRY: Yeah, I think I better go.

BOBBY: So you never told me. How's Judy?

LARRY: We went out a couple of times.

BOBBY: Was it good?

LARRY: I thought so, yeah. We talked. She does lapidary as a hobby.

LYNETTE: What's lapidary?

LARRY: The art of polishing rocks, you know, to make them smooth, bring out the color.

LYNETTE: It's called lapidary?

LARRY: Yeah. That's what she's into.

BOBBY: You go to bed with her?

LARRY: Not yet.

BOBBY: Uh-huh. *(Bobby takes Lynette's arm and starts stroking the skin on the inside.)*

BOBBY: You kiss her yet?

LARRY: Well yeah, we've done some kissing.

BOBBY: *(Stroking Lynette's arm.)* So, was it good?

LYNETTE: *(Smacking Bobby.)* Bobby, don't.

> *(Bobby holds on to Lynette's arm and buries his face in the crook of her elbow, making little nibbles with his lips.)*

LYNETTE: *(Giggling and screaming.)* Bobby, c'mon. Larry tell him to stop.

BOBBY: I love your skin, Lynette.

LYNETTE: It tickles! C'mon, stop! Larry, tell him to stop!

LARRY: *(Resigned.)* Stop.

> *(Bobby and Lynette wrestle each other in the booth, smacking and tickling each other. Larry plays with the wrapper from his straw.)*

BOBBY: *(Over this.)* Come on, lemme touch your arm.

LYNETTE: Get outta here!

BOBBY: *(To Larry.)* She has skin like an angel. I wanna touch it all over.

LYNETTE: Larry, tell him to stop!

BOBBY: I wanna crawl into it and fall asleep.

LARRY: I'm gonna go.

LYNETTE: Larry, no. You don't hafta.

BOBBY: Larry, hang out.

LYNETTE: Come on, hang out.

LARRY: *(Getting up.)* No, I'm gonna go.

BOBBY: You didn't finish about Judy.

LARRY: That's OK.

LYNETTE: Larry, stay.

LARRY: Nah, I'm gonna go. I'll see you around, OK?

BOBBY: What're you doing tomorrow?

LARRY: I dunno. I'll call you.

LYNETTE: You wanna talk, call me, OK?

LARRY: OK. Thanks for the Coke.

(*Larry leaves. They sit for a beat. Bobby makes a half-hearted attempt to stroke Lynette's arm.*)

LYNETTE: (*Truly annoyed.*) Don't.

(*A long beat. Bobby finishes the rest of Lynette's pizza. Lynette folds designs in the straw wrapper. Finally:*)

BOBBY: You want me to get you something else?

LYNETTE: No.

BOBBY: You wanna go?

LYNETTE: I don't care.

(*They both stare at the table for another beat. Neither one has anything to say to the other.*)

BOBBY: (*Finally.*) OK, let's get outta here.

(*They get up as the lights fade.*)

END OF PLAY

Keeper
by Frederick Bailey

CHARACTERS

MITSUKO

WILKINSON

STRADLING

PLACE

The lobby of an off-off-Broadway-type waiver theater in Los Angeles. The entrance from the outside is on stage right—there's a parking lot out there. The box office, just inside the door, is not much more than a high desk behind a railing, with a telephone. A side table of refreshments sits at up center, with a forty-cup coffee urn, sugar, creamer, honey, mustard, ketchup, salt and pepper. A digital clock over the box office reads just after seven PM. Posters from previous productions adorn the walls. The entrance to the theater itself is a set of double doors up a corridor at up left. A person could stand in the corridor and not be seen from the box office.

TIME

Tomorrow night.

Keeper

Mitsuko, a Japanese-American woman in her thirties, enters down the corridor carrying a cash box and a reservation book. She's dressed in a nice-looking skirt and blouse and high heels. She's going to be taking care of the box office tonight. She empties a lobby ashtray into a wastebasket as she circles behind the high desk. She starts arranging her book and box. The telephone rings.

MITSUKO: *(On the phone.)* Catapult Theatreworks, this is Mitzi… Hi, Charlie… Yeah… We got about ninety-five on the books for tonight. Four walk-ups and we're sold out… What *about* the coffee?… She's not?… But I'm running the box office tonight. I can't do both… All right, all right, I'll do it now. Okay? Just calm down. Nobody's here yet. I'm doing it right now. When are you getting here?… So I'm supposed to handle everything by myself until intermission? Thanks a bunch.
(Mitsuko hangs up, hurriedly plucks the box office cash out of the cash box, folds the wad of bills, puts it in her pocket, starts to pick up the coffee urn from the side table when Wilkinson comes in through the front entrance.)

MITSUKO: Oh, you're early. We're not really open yet. The play doesn't start until eight. *(Something about the odd way he smiles at her makes her hesitate.)* You're here for the play, aren't you?

WILKINSON: Not exactly. I guess so. What's it called?

MITSUKO: *Tie Goes to the Runner.*

WILKINSON: What's it about?

MITSUKO: I'm in kind of a rush. Have you got a reservation?

WILKINSON: No.

MITSUKO: Well, we've only got four seats left, so you'd better make up your mind.

WILKINSON: What's your name?

MITSUKO: Mitzi.

WILKINSON: Don't I know you from somewhere? You're a TV star.

MITSUKO: I don't think so.

WILKINSON: You look like one.

MITSUKO: I'll be right back. Don't go away.

WILKINSON: I won't.

> (*Mitsuko leaves in a hurry with the coffee urn. Wilkinson takes out a note-pad, makes notes, pacing the lobby, relaxed, unworried. He hears a vehicle drive up outside, tires crunching on gravel. He glances out the front door. He double-takes. He's shocked at what he sees. He's rattled. He looks around, calms himself, trying to figure out what he wants to do, what angle to play. He gets an idea. He looks to see if Mitsuko is coming back. It would appear she's not. He sits behind the box office desk, perching on a high stool, as though he were the box-office personnel. Stradling comes in the front entrance, looking around. He's pleased to see he's the only other person here. Stradling is an average guy in his thirties, dressed in jeans and sports jacket for a night out. Wilkinson is a slightly older guy in a good suit. He's easygoing and charming.*)

STRADLING: Hi.

WILKINSON: Hello.

STRADLING: I have a reservation.

WILKINSON: That's good. What name?

STRADLING: Stradling.

WILKINSON: For one person? (*Is there a faint touch of derision in Wilkinson's voice as he says that? Stradling nods, vaguely defensive, as he pulls out his wallet.*) One early bird…

> (*Wilkinson locates Stradling's name in the book, checks it off.*)

STRADLING: How much are the tickets?

WILKINSON: Ummm… (*He finds a flyer for the production.*) Twelve dollars. (*Stradling gives him a twenty. Wilkinson doesn't know the box office procedure, since he's playing it by ear. He fumbles with the cash box, but there's nothing in it except stray pieces of paper and a pencil. Wilkinson continues, referring to the twenty.*) Got anything smaller?

STRADLING: (*Shakes his head.*) Sorry. (*Wilkinson pulls out his own wallet and gives Stradling his change. He puts the twenty in the cash box.*) Thanks. You got a program?

> (*Wilkinson looks, finds a stack of programs, hands one to Stradling.*)

WILKINSON: Enjoy the play.

STRADLING: I'm sure I will. Did that review in the *Times* hurt your business any? (*Wilkinson shrugs noncommittally.*) Fuck the *Times*, huh? It got a great review in the *Reader*.

> (*Stradling wanders off across the lobby, talking inaudibly to himself, generally happy and pleased, but still—there's something gnawing at him around the edges. Wilkinson just sits in the box office, eyeballing Stradling but pretending not to.*)

STRADLING: Excuse me. Was there a guy in here, just before I came in the door?

WILKINSON: A guy? No.

STRADLING: Maybe ten minutes ago?

WILKINSON: Nobody. You're the first one here.

STRADLING: You're sure about that?

WILKINSON: Uh-huh.

STRADLING: Absolutely sure?

WILKINSON: Yes.

STRADLING: Good. That's good.

(Stradling wanders aside. Wilkinson looks worried now, but he covers it up.)

WILKINSON: Why do you want to know?

STRADLING: Because that means I got here before he did.

WILKINSON: *(Gives him a blank look.)* Before who?

STRADLING: My keeper. See, it's always like this. I'm on my way here. Or wherever I'm going. I'm in the truck driving. *He* gets here first. Before me. He comes in, goes around to all the women in the lobby and tells them I never wash my genitals. Then he leaves. Two minutes later, I walk in, I don't know he's been here. I got no idea. And all the women look at me. "He doesn't wash his genitals. Yucchhhh." And I can't figure out why nobody wants to talk to me.

WILKINSON: Who's this guy?

STRADLING: Just some keeper. I don't know if it's a man. It could be a woman.

(Wilkinson chuckles as though amused at a whimsical children's story.)

WILKINSON: What does he or she look like?

STRADLING: How would I know? He's always gone before I arrive. I thought if I got here first tonight, he'd come in, he'd see me here, he'd split. Nobody would have this advance negative word on me. Maybe I could meet somebody. The part that really murders me is it's not true. I shower daily.

WILKINSON: I don't get it. Why would he or she do this?

STRADLING: It's an experiment. Probably a government experiment.

WILKINSON: *(Laughs.)* So you're a walking guinea pig. Don't you think that's a little…?

STRADLING: A little what?

WILKINSON: I don't know.

STRADLING: Weird? Goofball?

WILKINSON: I wasn't going to say that. What kind of experiment?

STRADLING: "Individual effects of prolonged isolation in an ongoing social context." *(Wilkinson laughs indulgently, but underneath it he's really unnerved.)* Every once in a while he loses track of me. I get loose and I meet someone. And I wake up in the morning and she's there. Beside me. Oh man. I'm so relieved. For a few weeks I can wake up in the middle of the night and I'm not alone. But then somehow or other, I can't figure out how he does it. He finds me. And one day when I'm gone, he comes in and he tells the woman, "You don't know this guy, he's an asshole and a dumb shit," and then he fucks her and splits. I get home, and I say, "How are you, baby?" and she gets pissed off. She says, "You always ask me that." Couple of weeks later and she's gone. I can't figure out what happened. I'm sick of it.

WILKINSON: If you examine this, it doesn't make any real sense. If you've never seen the person, how do you know he exists? How do you know what he or she tells people about you if you're not there?

STRADLING: Things get back to me.

WILKINSON: It doesn't add up. You should talk to somebody about this.

STRADLING: You think I'm paranoid?

WILKINSON: Maybe you could use it as a stand-up routine in one of those open mike clubs, you know? One of those comedy places. You could develop it. I think it's good material.

(Mitsuko comes back through the double doors, carrying the coffee urn. It's heavy.)

STRADLING: Let me help you with that.

MITSUKO: Oh. Thanks.

STRADLING: Where's it going?

MITSUKO: On the table.

(They place it on the side table. Stradling smiles at her. She smiles back, but then she notices Wilkinson sitting behind the desk. She gives him an odd look—she doesn't know what he's doing there. Wilkinson moves aside deferentially. Both Stradling and Wikinson watch her as Mitsuko gets down under the table and plugs the coffee urn into a socket. They exchange a silent look. She stands, dusting off her hands. She goes behind the desk.)

WILKINSON: Mr. Stradling's money is in the till. I gave him a program.

MITSUKO: *(Not sure how to react.)* You took his money?

WILKINSON: Uh-huh. I won't be watching the show tonight. Not if there's only four seats left.

(Wilkinson's implying he's seen it before, as if he were part of the staff. Mitsuko is puzzled, but Wilkinson has a certain charm.)

MITSUKO: Okay.

(Mitsuko takes the twenty out of the cash box, wondering what's going on with these two men, wondering if she should be worried. Stradling stands perfectly still.)

WILKINSON: I gave him his change.

STRADLING: *(Stiffly, to Wilkinson.)* Where's the bathroom?

(Wilkinson points vaguely.)

MITSUKO: Through the doors, on the right.

(Stradling nods, as though he's just had his suspicions confirmed. He goes off through the double doors. Wilkinson makes sure Stradling has left. He turns back to Mitsuko in the box office, with his back to the double doors. Stradling sneaks back out, crouching in the corridor where Wilkinson can't see him.)

WILKINSON: *(To Mitsuko.)* You know what that guy just said? *(He looks over his shoulder, but doesn't see Stradling.)* He told me he never washes his genitals.

MITSUKO: *(Disgusted.)* Why not?

WILKINSON: Said he doesn't believe in it. Some kind of religious cult or something. Weird, huh?

STRADLING: *Liar!*

(Stradling attacks Wilkinson. They struggle ferociously, knocking the coffee urn off the table, spilling water and coffee grounds. Mitsuko screams.)

MITSUKO: *Stop it! Stop it!*

(They fight. Stradling forces Wilkinson down against the up center wall between the box office and the side table. Stradling pulls out a big knife. Wilkinson screeches in terror. Stradling plunges the knife into Wilkinson's belly. Mitsuko gasps in horror. Wilkinson is now frozen in shock. Stradling slowly draws the blade out. He stabs Wilkinson with it two more times, fast, then jumps back into a fierce stance with a frightening howl. Mitsuko screams. She starts for the door. Stradling moves lithely, interceding so she can't get out. But he doesn't touch her. He only smiles at her, hiding the knife behind his back. Mitsuko grabs the phone, punches 911. Stradling calmly takes the phone out of her hand and hangs it up. He gives her a gentle smile. Mitsuko stares back at him, swallowing her terror. Wilkinson feels his stomach. He's not dead. He's not even wounded. He makes desperate gasping sounds, happy to be alive. Stradling nods toward Wilkinson, indicating to Mitsuko that she should take a look. She realizes Wilkinson is unharmed.)

MITSUKO: Are you all right? *(Stradling takes the plastic ketchup dispenser off the side table and squirts ketchup all over Wilkinson. Wilkinson screws up his face. Mitsuko looks at Stradling.)* What are you doing? Are you *nuts?*

(Stradling demonstrates to both of them that it's a collapsible knife—the

blade retracts into the handle. Stradling shrugs. Wilkinson scrambles up and rushes out the front door. Stradling smiles at Mitsuko.)

STRADLING: Come on. I'll help you clean this up. You got a mop?

MITSUKO: I ought to call the cops.

STRADLING: Guy's been spreading lies about me. I had enough. I had to show him. What would you have done? *(He offers her the phone.)* My life is in your hands.

(Mitsuko takes the phone.)

MITSUKO: That's the most incredible line of bullshit I've ever heard.

(Mitsuko hangs up the phone.)

STRADLING: It's not a line. It's the truth.

MITSUKO: I believe you. *(She crosses away from him.)* It's still a line.

(She opens a narrow broom closet and takes out a bucket and mop.)

STRADLING: I guess anything a man says to a woman is a line. What's your name?

(She looks at him strangely. Long, motionless pause while she thinks about answering.)

MITSUKO: My name is Mitsuko.

(She tosses him the mop. He catches it. They smile at each other.)

END OF PLAY

Lawyers, Guns, & Money
by Thad Davis

CHARACTERS

FORD: A man in his twenties.

KEVIN: A man in his twenties.

LYDIA: A woman in her twenties.

PLACE

Kevin's apartment.

A note on the handgun: A nine-millimeter automatic really would be best. Having said that, a revolver will do in a pinch. If the choice is made to go with a revolver, please make the following changes:

Change Ford's "European automatic" to ".357 Magnum" or ".38 Special" or whatever kind of handgun is being used.

Change Kevin's "That nine-millimeter pistol you're holding…" to "That six-shot revolver you're holding…"

Finally, adjust all the prices (Guesses, actual, wholesale, retail, etc.) downward by about a third.

Lawyers, Guns, & Money

Ford, Kevin, and Lydia having drinks.

FORD: Lydia, leaving the program took courage.

KEVIN: ...to stare the Emperor in the eye and call him naked.

LYDIA: I'm frightened. I want to do good, but—

KEVIN: But? There's something else.

FORD: The ancients speak of glory.

LYDIA: Sometimes, I want to be like Ford.

FORD: Aha.

KEVIN: No. Not "aha."

FORD: No, Lydia, I think you're on to something.

KEVIN: We all sometimes want to be like Ford. That's the point. His life, and the lives of those like him, are temptations, like cocaine, or being a gangster.

FORD: A gangster?

LYDIA: You want to be a gangster?

KEVIN: No, I don't want to be a gangster. But part of me does. A small part of me finds it tempting.

LYDIA: Gangster like a gang-banger, or gangster like the Mafia?

KEVIN: Like the Mafia. But my point is, when you examine the fantasy closely you see that it is not, in fact, something you would actually want. Like being a lawyer, like Ford.

LYDIA: I thought you wanted to be a Beastie Boy?

KEVIN: I do. That's not a temptation though, it's simply unrealistic. Given the chance, I would drop everything to be a Beastie Boy, with no moral qualms whatsoever.

FORD: Me too, I would drop everything if I could be a Beastie Boy.

LYDIA: Well maybe there's my answer.

KEVIN: I feel like you're mocking me now. Which is fine. But I would hope that you would steer clear of my hopes and dreams and confine your ridicule to what I do.

FORD: Which would be...what?

LYDIA: Hope and dream?

KEVIN: There we go. That's more like it. Pretend that I don't actually do anything worth talking about.

FORD: But Kevin, you don't. When we ask you what you've been up to, you never talk about your job. It's not important to you, why should it be important to us?

LYDIA: You're still doing temp work, right?

KEVIN: Yes.

FORD: Kevin, we take our cues from you.

LYDIA: Do you like it?

KEVIN: No. But it's very very easy.

FORD: Well okay then.

KEVIN: I'm going to show you something.

FORD: A new tattoo?

KEVIN: It will surprise you, and you might be a little upset.

LYDIA: I don't want to see it.

KEVIN: It's okay, it's nothing gross. It's...well, a handgun.

(Kevin lays a handgun on the table.)

LYDIA: Oh, Kevin.

FORD: Kevin, it's okay. We love you—

KEVIN: Okay, this is what I was trying to avoid. Here, it's unloaded. Touch it.

LYDIA: I'm leaving.

FORD: Wait. Kevin, what's the matter? What's going on?

LYDIA: Kevin, I respect your temp work.

KEVIN: I'm going to stand up—

FORD: Oh, God—

KEVIN: —and step away from the gun. The gun will be by itself, unloaded. And therefore it will not hurt us. *(Kevin stands up and steps away from the gun.)* Let's all breathe. *(They breathe.)* Ford, Lydia, I have a business proposition.

LYDIA: You *are* a gangster.

FORD: A heist. You're planing a heist and you're letting us in. Damn.

KEVIN: No heist. What I'm proposing is completely legal. In fact, if anything seems otherwise, *Ford*, I'd like you to tell me.

LYDIA: You are shrewd.

FORD: Already planning your defense. Attorney client privilege.

KEVIN: How much do you think this cost?

FORD: Is it hot?

LYDIA: Two hundred dollars.

KEVIN: No, I purchased it legally, retail. There was a waiting period, and I have a permit.

LYDIA: Three hundred.

KEVIN: Ford?

FORD: Let me see it.

(Ford picks up the gun.)

LYDIA: Ford!

KEVIN: It's okay. What do you think?

FORD: European automatic. I'm assuming it's not counterfeit. Twelve hundred.

KEVIN: I paid eight hundred dollars for this.

FORD: What are you going to do with it?

LYDIA: Ford, put it down.

KEVIN: Let Lydia hold it.

LYDIA: No!

KEVIN: C'mon, give it a try.

FORD: C'mon, Lydia.

LYDIA: Why, what for?

KEVIN: Because you can. Because it's your right. Like voting, or freely practicing your religion.

LYDIA: I think the Second Amendment is suspect as written, and even more so as interpreted. I favor strict gun laws.

KEVIN: So do I, Lydia.

FORD: Don't we all?

LYDIA: Are you proposing we form a well-regulated militia?

KEVIN: Take the gun, Lydia. It's not loaded.

LYDIA: That's the oldest mistake in the book.

KEVIN: That's just the kind of smart, responsible thinking that makes me comfortable giving you a gun.

FORD: It's pretty nice, Lydia. It's surprisingly heavy.

KEVIN: Take it. Handle it as if it were loaded.

(Lydia takes the gun.)

FORD: There we go.

KEVIN: It looks good, Lydia. How does it feel?

LYDIA: Okay. It has heft. It's like a machine.

KEVIN: What do you think that cost wholesale?

LYDIA: I don't know about things like that. Seven hundred?

FORD: Three, four hundred.

KEVIN: This weapon wholesales for about five hundred dollars.

FORD: You're going to sell them to gangsters from the trunk of your car. There's a shipment waiting at the border. Am I right?

LYDIA: Kevin, that's bad.

FORD: Nasty.

LYDIA: What would happen if I pulled the trigger?

FORD: Don't.

KEVIN: Well, remember we're operating on the new assumption that this gun *is* loaded. But even if it weren't, it's not a good idea to pull the trigger. It's bad for the gun.

LYDIA: Like an empty coffee pot on a hot burner?

FORD: That's an excellent analogy.

KEVIN: Yes, not the end of the world, but neither is it a good idea. Ford, there will be no selling of guns to gangsters. And the whole "trunk of my car" bit seems a little sordid. But, I am proposing that we get into the gun business.

LYDIA: Like open a store?

KEVIN: Are you guys familiar with the term "multilevel distribution"?

FORD: Oh, Kevin.

KEVIN: Your reaction is completely understandable.

LYDIA: What's multilevel distribution?

FORD: Try pyramid scheme.

KEVIN: Technically, pyramid schemes are illegal. Now—

LYDIA: What, is this like, what's the name of that company—

KEVIN: Don't say it.

LYDIA: My cousin tricked me into going to a meeting, then I had to buy a bunch of soap and bad gum.

FORD: You set us up. This whole get-together-for-drinks was all a setup so that you could get us into your cult. You're going to bring in some guy who'll "let us in on an opportunity."

KEVIN: There's no cult.

FORD: Some sort of pyramid gun cult.

LYDIA: I feel dirty. You made me hold the gun. That's a trick they tell you to do.

KEVIN: There's no they. This is me. My idea. Yes, there's a pyramid, or there will be, but it's ours. We're at the top.

FORD: Selling guns?

KEVIN: Yes. To our friends. And at the same time encouraging them to do likewise. We make money from what we sell, and more importantly, we get a cut from what they sell, and so on and so on. Exponentially. Like a pyramid.

LYDIA: Because of multiplication.

KEVIN: Yes.

FORD: We don't exactly hang with the gun crowd, Kevin.

KEVIN: That's the point. The people we know wouldn't dream of walking into a gun store. But most of them, if given a chance, privately, would be thrilled to handle a firearm. And would be surprised to know that they could afford one.

LYDIA: Guns are inherently dangerous.

FORD: The world's inherently dangerous.

LYDIA: Statistically a gun is more likely to be used against its owner than in actual defense of the owner.

KEVIN: Statistically, a person is more likely to believe in alien abductions than they are to vote. I trust myself and my judgment, and I'm counting on my friends to do likewise.

FORD: Would you sell to Jake?

KEVIN: Jake Ingram? Sure.

FORD: But what about his wife?

KEVIN: What about her?

LYDIA: She's heavily medicated. And she breaks things in anger.

KEVIN: Right. I would caution Jake to consider his domestic situation, as I would anyone, particularly households with children. I would encourage him to purchase a trigger lock and lockbox, but ultimately the decision would be his.

FORD: It could be complicated, legally.

KEVIN: Dealer permits are cheap and easy to get. And there's a conceal-and-carry bill before the legislature that if passed—

FORD: —could blow this thing wide open, right. But I'm a little concerned about the lack of potential for repeat business.

KEVIN: Don't be. Once you buy one, you'll find yourself wanting more. This is my third. Talk to me, Lydia.

LYDIA: I feel ashamed.

FORD: Shame's unhealthy. That's your momma talking.

LYDIA: My mother is righteous, enlightened, and liberated. This would break her heart.

KEVIN: Lydia, I respect your mother. I respect the work she's done. ERA, pro-choice, childcare, all of that has been about options and self-determination for women. That nine-millimeter pistol you're holding, that's just another step. That's just another set of options that traditionally women have been denied but which are legally and morally theirs by right. Your mother wasn't afraid to shock her mother. And she didn't raise you to be afraid to shock her.

(Pause.)

LYDIA: I could sell her one.

KEVIN: Give it to her as a gift, with lessons.

LYDIA: Sometimes nasty is good.

FORD: So, is this a scam or a legitimate business?

KEVIN: We're at the top of the pyramid, I don't think it has to be either/or. We're selling a quality product, aggressively.

LYDIA: What are we selling? Guns?

FORD: Security.

LYDIA: Or the pyramid?

KEVIN: Opportunity.

LYDIA: Power.

FORD: Power.

KEVIN: Without that, you can't really be said to have it all, now can you?

FORD: Lydia.

LYDIA: Yes, Ford?

FORD: Are you still afraid?

LYDIA: No. Not at all.

(Lydia pulls the trigger, the gun goes off. Pause. Everyone bursts into laughter.)

FORD: Yeah.

KEVIN: I'm going to get me a big-ass Suburban—dark green, bulletproof.

END OF PLAY

Hard-Boiled
by Deborah Lynn Frockt

CHARACTERS

JACKSON: Man, mid-twenties.
MICKEY: Man, mid-twenties.
KRAMER: Woman, mid-twenties.

TIME AND PLACE

The present.
A bar.

Hard-Boiled

In a bar, on a Friday night. After a very long week. The guys are checking things out. Used shot glasses, sucked-up lemon rinds, and salt abound. Jackson and Mickey sit at a table for three with the sounds of a popular hot spot buzzing around them.

JACKSON: Hot.

MICKEY: Scorching.

JACKSON: Like an iron.

MICKEY: Like the equator.

JACKSON: Too hot to handle.

MICKEY: Hot mama.

JACKSON: Hot.

MICKEY: Way hot.

JACKSON: A babe.

MICKEY: A total babe.

JACKSON: A totally babalicious babe.

MICKEY: A totally babalicious babe with ultimate babocity.

JACKSON: A totally babalicious babe with ultimate babocity, who looks like she comes from…

JACKSON AND MICKEY: *(Together.)* Babalonia!

(Kramer approaches the table. She is dressed to kill and very, very sexy. Yet professional. She has a total sense of her body and does her best to maximize all her best features, which are probably all her features. Kramer has a whole bottle of Cuervo. She hums the whole tune of "Tequila" pouring shots for all. She keep humming until they're in position ready to shoot the tequila which they do, then:)

ALL: Tequila!

JACKSON: Kramer, you shouldn't be buying your own congratulatory cocktails. 'Specially not a whole bottle of Gold.

MICKEY: Hey, she's the one who can best afford it now. Throw down, Junior Associate!

KRAMER: That's *Ms.* Junior Associate to you, cowboy!

MICKEY: Attitude. Attitude.

KRAMER: Hey man, it takes you places. It takes you places you want to be.

MICKEY: You've got it, babe. No doubt about it. No doubt about anything at all now.

JACKSON: So what's it feel like? What's it really feel like to know what's next, exactly where you're goin', and how many k's a year you'll be doin'? What's the secret agenda now that you're in?

MICKEY: Hey, James Bond, who needs a secret agenda? Who needs an agenda at all? The agenda was…get the job…do pass go, do collect $200. Kramer's got the paycheck, man, fuck the power.

KRAMER: Power is…a nice…idea.

JACKSON: Aren't the words power and nice in close proximity to each other in a sentence, kinda like oxymoronic?

KRAMER: I think you've got a point, counselor.

MICKEY: He's sharp as nails. Deer-in-the-headlights look, but hey, Holmes is in the know. I guess he doesn't know whatever it is you know, but then again, neither do I.

KRAMER: You guys know plenty.

JACKSON: Plenty, but not quite enough.

MICKEY: Down, boy.

KRAMER: Give the girl a break. Pals? Remember?

JACKSON: I'm sorry, Kramer. That was out of line. This is your celebration, your congratulation drink…um drinks. Pals!

KRAMER: Cheers?

JACKSON: Cheers! *(Addressing Mickey.)* Hey…worm brain…cheers!

MICKEY: Oh yeah yeah yeah. Cheers.

KRAMER: Whatcha thinkin' about, Mickey?

MICKEY: Thinkin' what a ball-buster this year's been.

KRAMER: Damn straight.

MICKEY: Oh, come on Kramer. There isn't any way you can convince me you've got balls under that sexy suit. Junior associate or no junior associate.

KRAMER: I not only have 'em Mickster, they're in mint condition. No worse for wear. How 'bout you, Jax?

JACKSON: Black and blue but not busted. Never busted.

MICKEY: You sure talk a tough game, lady.

KRAMER: Play or pay, man, play or pay. That's what they taught me at lawyer school.

JACKSON: Attitude?

KRAMER: Attitude.

MICKEY: You've got a mouth that won't quit.

KRAMER: I'm a lawyer, Mick.

JACKSON: A junior associate lawyer at a major, major, very major firm.

MICKEY: Kramer, we've got the JD/MBA's, same as you. Just the same as you.

JACKSON: Mickey.

KRAMER: It's okay. Mickey, we've all got 'em. We all know that. And we all knew it when they brought us on board.

JACKSON: The three stooges. Remember, Mick. Harvard, Penn, and Stanford. Woob, woob, woob.

MICKEY: The hot rods.

KRAMER: Ooh ouch.

JACKSON: Sizzlin'.

(They drink.)

MICKEY: So how do you think they did it?

JACKSON: What? The Cubans and Kennedy? Again with the assassination, Mick?

MICKEY: Smart ass. How'd the partners settle on bachelorette number two?

JACKSON: The lovely and talented, Mizzzzzzzzz Sherry Kramer.

MICKEY: Lovely. She certainly is lovely. You certainly are lovely, Ms. Sherry Kramer.

KRAMER: Why, Mickey, how you do make a girl blush.

MICKEY: Chicks with balls don't blush.

JACKSON: Now, if I've told you once, I've told you a million times, Mickey. Nobody with a JD/MBA is a chick.

MICKEY: She dresses like a chick. She smells like a chick. And she sure as hell moves like a chick.

KRAMER: It's true. You've found me out. I'm not just a JD/MBA. I'm a *female* JD/MBA.

MICKEY: Hey sweetheart, no man in this office has ever doubted *that* for a second.

KRAMER: Mick, cut the sweetheart shit.

MICKEY: Hey, Jax. Don't you wonder? Don't you wonder just a little bit how they distinguished between Larry, Moe, and Curly?

JACKSON: Well, Curly's the bald one. Everybody knows that, Mickey.

MICKEY: But we've all got our hair, Jax. How'd they do it with these stooges? Mickey, Jax, and Kramer. All the best schools. All law review. All the highest honors. All working eighty, ninety hours a week. No doubt, all three…the brightest and the best.

JACKSON: Mickey, we always knew, from right when we started, we always knew they'd only take one of us.

MICKEY: And we had one year. One year only to stand out, to really shine. To see if we'd make it, if we'd be the one.

KRAMER: That's right. We all came in with the same chance.

JACKSON: And one of us got the job. And that's what we're here celebrating.

MICKEY: Throwin' 'em back at Bob's, just like we always do.

JACKSON: Like we always do. Together.

KRAMER: Checkin' out the scene.

MICKEY: Kramer, man. You're not a guy. You're not one of us. You can fanta-size all you want about havin' balls in your Victoria Secret panties, but what everyone notices are the tits in your Ann Taylor blouse.

JACKSON: Jesus, Mickey. What the fuck is the matter with you?

MICKEY: What the fuck is the matter with me? What the fuck is the matter with me? What the fuck is the matter with you? She fuckin' got the job. Now, how in the hell did she do it? We're all the same. We're like fucking identical triplets on paper and in performance. But one of us has got an ass that won't quit under her pinstripes.

KRAMER: You're outta line. You're way outta line, Mickey.

MICKEY: No, I'll tell you what's out of line. What's out of line is that every partner in this office gets a hard-on the size of the Fifth Circuit docket when you walk by. You wanna talk about what distinguishes the stooges? Nobody ever wanted to get in Curly's pants the way they want to get in yours.

JACKSON: Let's go, Kramer. Let's get out of here.

MICKEY: Oh, siddown and cool your jets, Jackson. I'll be the one to go. I mean, I am the one way out of line here. But don't you get all fuckin' high and mighty, homey. You check her ballsy ass out too. You check it out the same as the rest of the boy lawyers with moveable parts. And don't think she doesn't know it either. Congratulations, Kramer. What did you do in that ninety-first hour anyway? *(Mickey exits.)*

JACKSON: He didn't mean it. We've all had too much to drink.

KRAMER: Yeah. We sure have, haven't we?

JACKSON: It's just hard for him right now. I know he didn't mean it.

KRAMER: No. We're pals. We're colleagues. We made it through…together.

JACKSON: Balls intact.

KRAMER: All six of 'em.

JACKSON: Unfuckingbreakable.

KRAMER: Do you check me out, Jax?

JACKSON: You're really beautiful, Kramer.

KRAMER: Do you think about fucking me, Jax?

JACKSON: Um, not always, but I mean sometimes, sure, I've thought what it might be like if we, you know, if we…

KRAMER: Do you think about fucking me, Jax?

JACKSON: Yeah.

KRAMER: You think they think about it, Jax? You think they think about what it would be like to have a junior associate they wanted to fuck?

JACKSON: I gotta go, Kramer. I gotta go, 'cause…

KRAMER: 'Cause it's time to go.

JACKSON: I'll call you tomorrow. *(Jackson pats her on the back awkwardly and exits.)*

KRAMER: Yeah. Bye. *(Kramer pours a drink. After a long pause, she downs it.)* Tequila.

END OF PLAY

Eye to Eye
by Christopher Graybill

CHARACTERS
MAN

WOMAN

WAITER

TIME AND PLACE
A restaurant. Present.

Eye to Eye

As the play opens, the Man and Woman have finished dinner at a fashionable restaurant. He reaches across the table toward her hand, though he does not touch her, and gazes into her eyes.

WOMAN: That's enough.

MAN: What's enough?

WOMAN: Stop, please.

MAN: Stop what?

WOMAN: Looking at me.

MAN: I like looking at you.

WOMAN: I can see that.

MAN: Don't you like it?

WOMAN: Sort of.

MAN: You like it. You love it.

WOMAN: Up to a point.

MAN: Set by you?

WOMAN: Who else?

    (Beat.)

MAN: So you don't like my looks. I like yours. There are flecks of brown in your right eye. Did you know that?

WOMAN: Yes.

MAN: They are very beautiful, your eyes.

WOMAN: Only the part you can see. My eyeballs are red-veined, elongated bulbs of jelly. Just like yours.

MAN: Please, I just ate. How come it bothers you? My looking at you. No, really. I'm interested.

WOMAN: It's too intimate.

MAN: Intimate? We're just sitting here. Having coffee. I'm way over here.

WOMAN: There's something in your eye.

MAN: What?

WOMAN: I can't quite recognize it.

MAN: Something in my eye. Let me see now. Is it a gnat?

WOMAN: No.

MAN: An eyelash?

WOMAN: It's something hidden.

MAN: Something warm? Something cool? Something sexy?

WOMAN: Not exactly.

MAN: Bedroom eyes?

WOMAN: More than that.

MAN: That's interesting. That's very, very interesting.

(Waiter enters.)

WAITER: How was everything this evening?

WOMAN: Fine, thank you.

MAN: Fascinating.

WAITER: Can I bring you anything else?

MAN: I'd like more coffee.

WOMAN: Just the check, please.

(Waiter nods and exits.)

MAN: You double-parked?

WOMAN: Hmmm.

(They sit briefly in silence until Waiter returns.)

WAITER: Here we are. *(He refills Man's cup and leaves check.)* I'll take that whenever you're ready. *(He exits.)*

WOMAN: *(Picking up check.)* I'll get this.

MAN: No, my treat. *(He snatches the check from her hand.)*

WOMAN: Why don't we split it?

MAN: No, no, no, no. I treat you, then you treat me. That's the way it works around here.

WOMAN: I really would rather…

MAN: You're welcome. *(He takes a credit card out of his wallet and places it on top of the bill.)* You can get it next time.

WOMAN: Wait a minute. You better let me split it now. There isn't going to be a next time.

(They look at each other a moment.)

MAN: I see. OK. Tell you what. I've got a deal for you.

WOMAN: No, thanks.

MAN: A sporting proposition.

WOMAN: How much is my half?

(During the following exchange, she repeatedly reaches for the check, and he holds it away.)

MAN: No, no. Let's do this fair and square. We both want to pay. We'll compete for it. Loser pays.

WOMAN: This is a boy's game.

MAN: We'll have a looking contest. Whoever breaks eye contact first, loses. *(Pause.)* Well?

WOMAN: Loser pays the check?

MAN: Bingo.

WOMAN: You're on. Ready?

MAN: Wait a minute. Let me get loose here. *(Does facial and neck exercises.)* The World Eyeballing Championships. All right. The Kid is ready. Here we go. On your mark, get set, stare!

WOMAN: *(Immediately averting her eyes.)* OK, I lose. Give me the check.

MAN: Oh, no. Time out.

WOMAN: I lost, fair and square. Hand it over.

MAN: No. I see what's happening here. I get it. We're going to have to revise the rules. *Winner* picks up the check.

WOMAN: I really want to leave.

MAN: Then leave! Walk out! Allow me the great honor of paying for you. Let me treat you. It would be my pleasure. *(Pause.)* Are you going to play or not?

WOMAN: I'll play.

(She takes out her credit card. They lay their gold American Express cards on the table.)

MAN: Ah, victory. Gold versus gold. At last we see eye to eye.

WOMAN: Just start.

MAN: Go!

(They begin.)

MAN: Ho, ho, what a glare. Daggers, bullets. You won't be able to keep that up for long. You know what you look like?

WOMAN: Do you have to talk?

MAN: Why not? Nobody said anything about talking. There's nothing in the rules about talking. As I was saying, you look like one of those gargoyles who can turn men to stone.

WOMAN: Gorgon.

MAN: What?

WOMAN: It's a Gorgon, not a gargoyle.

MAN: Well, you must be a Gorgon because you are definitely turning me to stone.

WOMAN: You feel something getting hard?

MAN: Absolutely.

WOMAN: Maybe it's your arteries.

MAN: Ho, ho. Very good. But you don't get any style points.

(Waiter enters, notices their intensity, and hesitates.)

WAITER: Can I take that for you? (No response.) No problem. Just let me know when you're ready. (He exits.)

MAN: Your eyes are quivering. You're blinking fast. It won't be long now. Any second now you'll lose it. Ha, you looked away.

WOMAN: I did not.

MAN: Almost. You will.

WOMAN: Everything is a covert operation with men, isn't it?

MAN: Don't lecture me about men.

WOMAN: All right, you. Let's talk about you. Nothing can be straightforward with you. It's all innuendo.

MAN: I never said that.

WOMAN: That's your secret weapon. You think what's unspoken is the biggest threat there is. But you're wrong.

MAN: Cheap shots. Nothing but cheap shots.

WOMAN: You never say what's on your mind.

MAN: How would you know?

WOMAN: I can see it in your eyes. Oh, it's not sex. I see that now. Sex is for teenagers. You're way past that.

MAN: What is it then?

WOMAN: I don't think you want me to say it.

MAN: Go ahead.

WOMAN: Not out loud.

MAN: As loud as you want.

WOMAN: Control. Domination. That's what's been in your eyes.

MAN: Is that the best you can do?

WOMAN: Sex is your means, not your end. (Louder.) You're thinking. I want to fuck this woman.

MAN: No fair.

WOMAN: (Louder.) I want to fuck her *into submission*.

WAITER: (Enters anxiously.) Are we OK here? Can I take that for you? Sir?

(Man looks up at Waiter.)

WOMAN: You lose.

(Man hesitates, holding the check. Then he reaches to take her credit card, and she hands it to him.)

MAN: Add 15 percent.

WOMAN: I'll tell him how much to add. Add 20 percent.

(Man gives him the check and a credit card, and Waiter exits.)

MAN: Don't gloat.

WOMAN: Why not? I won.

MAN: You had to cheat.

WOMAN: There are no rules.

MAN: You don't really believe that.

WOMAN: I told the truth. That's the ultimate weapon.

MAN: If you call truth a weapon, you are pretty far gone.

(Waiter returns with a salver holding credit card and invoice. He lays it beside Man and exits.)

WOMAN: You all stick together, don't you?

(She takes the invoice. He picks up the credit card off the tray and plays with it, as she bends to sign.)

MAN: Look me in the eye and tell me you're proud of what you did.

WOMAN: I am very, very proud. I thought this would be another night to forget. With another bitter, predictable prick. But I was wrong. I want to remember this. When my statement comes, I'm going to frame it and put it on my wall. Every time I look at it, I'll think of you. *(She signs the slip and tears off her copy.)* Could I have my card?

(He hands it to her.)

WOMAN: So long, loser. *(She exits.)*

(Man stares thoughtfully at his coffee. Waiter enters and picks up the credit card invoice.)

WAITER: Sir, there's some mix-up here. This isn't your signature.

MAN: I know.

WAITER: Your friend signed on *your* credit card?

MAN: She must have thought I gave you hers. She'll see her mistake when she gets her statement.

WAITER: Shall I run your card through again?

MAN: "There are no rules." Everybody says that. But they don't accept it. Not down deep. *(He tears up the credit slip and hands his card to Waiter.)* And do it right this time.

WAITER: Sir?

MAN: You added 25 percent. After she said 20. Make it 15. Exactly. Because I've got my eye on you.

END OF PLAY

Downtown
by Jeffrey Hatcher

CHARACTERS

BRETT

J

SASKIA

PLACE

A corner booth at a downtown club.

TIME

Very now. Very late in the evening.

Downtown

Preshow recording: Petula Clark singing "Downtown."*

As the house lights go down, the song plays through its first few bars, up to the end of the first reprise.

Scene: Lights come up on a cavernous black space. Smoke and noise. Sound of people jostling and mixing. One piece of furnishing on stage: a large, comfortable circular booth and dining table. Black leather. Seductive. The table is crowded with bottles and glasses. Cigarette smoke hangs over the booth. The flash of neon lights and the occasional strobe pulse glares through the smoke, tinting the scene in sickly pastels every few moments.

At rise: Three people are seated at the table. Brett, J, and Saskia. All in their mid- to late twenties. Very relaxed. Very poised. Brett is tall and lean. His hair is high, silky, and moussed. Black shirt buttoned at the top. Sunglasses. Cigarette in hand. J is small. Balding. A black T-shirt and overpadded black jacket. Sunglasses. Cigarette in hand. Saskia is an icy blonde, her hair in a vicious cut. Chalky skin. Purple black lipstick. Jewelry. Black T-shirt. Sunglasses. Cigarette in hand. All three are drawling over the minefield of bottles, champagne flutes, and cocktails that crowd the table. Behind their black sunglasses, their eyes are focused on one corner of the club—somewhere out front. As the lights come up on this Dante-esque scene, crashing, dark, rhythmic dance music thunders through the club's sound system. It is, of course, not so loud that it drowns the dialogue.

BRETT: Look at her.
J: *Look* at her.
SASKIA: I thought she was *dead*.
BRETT: Have you read her reviews?

---

*Cautionary Note: permission to produce this play does *not* include permission to use this song in production.

J: She's been dead for *years*.

BRETT: Look at that *outfit*.

J: The *way* that she *walks*....

BRETT: It's her all over....

J: And coming out the side.

BRETT: God, she's embarrassing.

J: Embarrassing, *please!*

SASKIA: *(Deadpan.)* There are so many ways she can embarrass herself it must be difficult to choose just one.

J: The hips, the boots, the hair....

BRETT: And that *outfit*.

SASKIA: She's like a tube of lipstick sweating gin.

BRETT: She's not a writer, she's an event.

J: Perhaps her critics haven't seen her best work yet.

SASKIA: There's nothing she has the critics haven't seen.

J: Casting aspersion on her private parts?

SASKIA: My dear, she *has* no private parts.

J: She's derivative.

SASKIA: She is.

J: Not like your stuff.

SASKIA: Not like *yours*.

J: She *steals* is what she does.

BRETT: She had one good book a long time ago, when was it, last year?

J: The one about nuns.

SASKIA: Lesbian nuns.

J: A modern version of *The Song of Bernadette*, only all the nuns were naked and without emotion.

SASKIA: Bold.

J: Right. Bold.

BRETT: Trés, trés, trés bold.

J: I used to shop where she shopped. Had the same sack of groceries every Friday. Nothing but cigarettes, condoms, and antidepressants.

SASKIA: It takes a lot to get through a weekend.

BRETT: She's dead.

SASKIA: She's dead.

J: Definitely. Dead. *(J looks back and forth between Brett and Saskia.)* Is it time? Is it time?

SASKIA: *(Deadpan, not looking at him.)* No. It's not time.

(They shift in their seats and look in another direction.)

BRETT: Check out the new boy.

SASKIA: He looks like a chauffeur.

BRETT: Look at his *out*fit! Is that a sharkskin suit?

J: I think it's a real shark's skin.

BRETT: *Look* at that *suit.* It's got a *reflection!* I can *see* myself in that suit.

J: You think it's too *much?*

SASKIA: Not if he had a gun and a partner with a gun.

J: What's his new book about?

BRETT: Probably another jaded, jaundiced, world-weary look at the glittering lifestyle, the pearl in the gutter, the cocaine and razor blades of the way-downtown scene.

SASKIA: A kind of modern *Madame Bovary*...

BRETT: A modern *La Bohème*...

SASKIA: A modern *Faust*...

J: Only the characters are all naked and without emotion.

BRETT: Its book club sales are doing *great* in Westchester.

J: Why not, he's derivative.

BRETT: Derivative.

J: Derivative is what he is.

BRETT: Not like *your* stuff.

J: No, not like *yours* either.

BRETT: He's dead.

SASKIA: He's dead.

J: Definitely. Dead.

(They shift again to look in another direction.)

J: Uh-oh.

BRETT: Uh-oh.

J: Enter the wunderkind.

BRETT: Oh, *my.*

J: What a *face!*

BRETT: What a *dresser!*

J: What a *charmer!*

SASKIA: What a *guy.*

BRETT: *(Beat. A lower voice.)* He's *such* a fraud.

J: He's *so* dis*gust*ing.

BRETT: So re*volt*ing.

J: He's the *worst.*

BRETT: The *absolute.*

J: The nadir of nadirs.

BRETT: A dis*a*ster without penultimate.

J: The stingiest…

BRETT: …the gaudiest…

SASKIA: He's looking this way.

> *(They all look up and blow "him" a kiss.)*

ALL: *(In unison.)* Kiss-kiss!

> *(They huddle in low voices again.)*

J: Did you read his latest?

BRETT: I didn't read it, I *lived* it.

J: Was it awful!

BRETT: It was like a week at the Men's Room at Grand Central.

SASKIA: Only naked…and without emotion.

J: I haven't seen him in the clubs recently.

BRETT: I haven't seen him in the clubs lately.

J: Some places won't let him in anymore.

BRETT: Some places bar the door.

SASKIA: I saw him at the opening of *Innertube*.

J: Really?

BRETT: What's *Innertube* like?

J: It opened last Thursday.

SASKIA: It's already dead.

BRETT: It's dead.

J: Everything's dead.

BRETT: Did you go to The Drainpipe's opening last night?

SASKIA: No, it's dead.

BRETT: *(Nods.)* It's dead.

J: Definitely. Dead.

BRETT: *(Looks out again.)* He's here with his agent.

SASKIA: Yes, he's here with The Dwarf.

J: Look at the Dwarf.

BRETT: He's like an endomorph.

J: He's like an exposed muscle.

SASKIA: He's like a hernia in a suit.

BRETT: He's gone downhill.

J: How can you tell?

BRETT: He used to represent movie stars.

J: He used to represent the best.

SASKIA: He used to represent Cheever and Updike, now he represents the decline of the West.

J: I wouldn't let him represent *my* stuff.

BRETT: I wouldn't let him represent *your* stuff either.

J: Nor yours.

SASKIA: Nor yours.

J: He's…he's….

BRETT: Derivative.

J: Derivative.

SASKIA: For an agent, he is.

J: Dead.

BRETT: Definitely. Dead.

J: *(Look to both of them.)* Is it time? Is it *time?*

SASKIA: *(Deadpan, not looking at him.)* No. It's not time.
    (They look in a different direction.)

BRETT: Look who's here now.

J: It's the *Vanity Fair* girls. The *nerve.*

BRETT: The *gall!*

SASKIA: *(Sing-song.)* Bitch-bitch-bitch, bitch-bitch-bitch…

J: *(Waspy.)* Oh, are there *six* of them?

BRETT: They came with Pajama.

J: Pajama?

BRETT: Pajama Dombrówicz.

SASKIA: Just wrote her bio. She's twenty-two. Called *Native New Yorker.*

BRETT: And like a lot of native New Yorkers, she's from Nebraska.

J: I think she's copied your stuff.

SASKIA: You *do?*

J: I think she's stolen your thunder.

SASKIA: You *do?*

J: I think she's plagiarized your best stuff from here to down under.

BRETT: But it's not *like* your stuff.

J: No, not *like* yours at all.

BRETT: She steals.

J: Yes, she steals.

BRETT: Yes, she steals from us all.

J: *(Looks at Brett.)* Not like your stuff.

BRETT: *(To J.)* Not like *your* stuff.

J: *(After a beat, to Brett.)* Well, actually, a *little* like your stuff.

BRETT: *(Blinks.)* Pardon?

J: Well, I mean…it's *kind* of like your stuff.

BRETT: That's what I said, she steals from us all.

J: Well….

BRETT: Well, what?

J: Well….

BRETT: *Well, what?*

J: You have the same views. You have the same concerns.

BRETT: Yes.

J: A similarity in style.

BRETT: Yes.

J: Subject matter.

BRETT: Yes.

J: Jokes….

BRETT: Yes.

J: …number of pages per book….

BRETT: Yes.

J: …preference for jacket covers….

BRETT: Yes, *so!*

J: Well…*she was* there *first.*

BRETT: *(A beat.)* Getting there *first* doesn't prove she didn't steal it from *me.*

J: But if she didn't steal it from you…*until* she started writing the same things that *you* wrote…then what did she steal if she wrote it first *before?*

BRETT: *(Biting off the words.)* She steals in retrospect. Are you suggesting *I* stole from *her?*

J: No!

BRETT: Are you suggesting I lifted styles?

J: No!

BRETT: Dialogue?

J: No!

BRETT: Characters?

J: No!

BRETT: Plots?

J: No….

BRETT: Well! All right then!

J: *(Thinks a beat.)* There *was* her first book….

BRETT: Yes….

J: Your first book….

BRETT: Yes….

J: It's a little like *her* first book.

BRETT: There are *no* similarities between *her* first book and *my* first book!

J: Of course not. *(Beat.)* Her first book got published.

BRETT: *My* first book was published!

J: No, it wasn't.

BRETT: Yes, it was!

J: It wasn't *sold*.

BRETT: *(Sputtering.)* It was bound!

J: It was *stapled*.

BRETT: Anything *else* I've stolen from her?

J: Uh, no, no, not you…. *(To Saskia.)* You, maybe, *(To Brett.)* but not you.

SASKIA: I beg your pardon.

J: Well….

SASKIA: What did I steal?

J: Well….

SASKIA: *Well what?*

J: Well, there was your second book.

SASKIA: My second book….

J: Your second book *was*…her *third* book.

SASKIA: My second book was her third book? Proves my point!

J: Except her *third* book came before your *second* book.

SASKIA: Her book was completely different!

J: From…?

SASKIA: From what?

J: Which book? All your books are alike.

SASKIA: *(Fuming.)* My second book was different from her third book!

J: Which came before your second.

SASKIA: *My* book was about a group of gay Khymer Rouge refugees who emigrate to South Africa to open a For-Profit Penal Colony run by lepers and dwarfs. *Her* book was about a group of gay Khymer Rouge refugees who emigrate to South Africa to open a For-Profit Penal Colony run by lepers and *midgets!* There *is* a *difference!*

J: I'm just saying there was similar subject matter.

BRETT: And style.

J: And dialogue.

BRETT: And opening lines…

J: And ending…

SASKIA: My book was a *meditation* on an earlier work!

BRETT: What earlier work?

J: *(Points at Pajama.)* Her third book.

SASKIA: It was a rethinking!

BRETT: *(Deadpan.)* It was a retyping.

J: We're not saying you stole.

BRETT: We're not saying you borrowed. *(Beat.)* We're not saying.

SASKIA: What are you implying?

BRETT: Why, what are you inferring?

SASKIA: If I infer what you're implying, then we know what the implications are.

BRETT: How do you know what we imply if you haven't already inferred what we imply?

J: Because she infers *first.*

SASKIA: I've never attacked *you!*

BRETT: I haven't attacked *you* either.

SASKIA: *(To J.)* And I haven't attacked you *either!*

J: No. No. No, you've *copied* me a little, but you haven't *attacked* me. Recently.

SASKIA: When did I attack you!

J: Well….

SASKIA: When did I attack you!

J: In print?

SASKIA: Yes, in print!

J: In print, never, no. No, never in print. They wouldn't print what you called an attack.

SASKIA: As if you've never criticized me!

J: Where?

SASKIA: In print!

J: In print?

BRETT: I wouldn't say he's never criticized you.

J: No.

SASKIA: No.

J: No.

SASKIA: When did you criticize me in print?

J: Well….

SASKIA: What did you publish?

J: It wasn't published.

SASKIA: It wasn't published!

J: I…*withheld* it from publication.

BRETT: That means he couldn't sell it.

SASKIA: The only way you could sell criticism of me would be if you put it on an umbrella and sold it in a rainstorm.

J: Plagiarist!

SASKIA: I don't plagiarize!

J: Neither do I!

BRETT: Neither do I!

SASKIA: I never steal anyone's dialogue!

BRETT: I never steal anyone's dialogue either!

SASKIA: Of course not!

BRETT: Of course not!

J: I have integrity!

BRETT: I have integrity!

J: As a journalist!

BRETT: As a journalist!

J: I have integrity! Yes!

BRETT: Yes! *(Beat.)* As a journalist?

J: What… ?

BRETT: A journalist?

SASKIA: Get a shovel….

J: I consider myself a journalist in the mode of Henry Adams, George Orwell, and Truman Capote!

SASKIA: That's only because Adams, Orwell, and Capote can't *sue.*

J: Who wrote the first articles on the Lower East Side?

SASKIA: Who wrote the first articles on attitude.

BRETT: And postmodernism!

SASKIA: And the club scene!

BRETT: And the galleries!

J: And the downtown world! *(Stand-off. They are all nose to nose. Beat.)* Well…well, it wasn't any of *us*, but who wrote them *next!* (They all look a bit shame-faced and uncomfortable.) Uh, is it time?

BRETT: *(Looks off.)* Shut up.

J: *(To Saskia.)* Is it time?

SASKIA: *(Moping.)* Shut up.

J: *(After a pause.)* I didn't mean to insult you.

SASKIA: *(Unconvinced.)* Sure.

J: *(To Brett.)* I didn't mean to insult *you.*

BRETT: *(Grumbling.)* Sure.

J: *(Looks back and forth for a moment.)* Is this gonna be the start of one of those famous literary feuds, like Mailer and Vidal?

SASKIA: Could be.

BRETT: It's a good guess.

SASKIA: Which do you want to be, Mailer or Vidal?

J: Because…we're probably more useful to one another if we stay together. In a union. In tandem. In concert. Solidarity.

BRETT: Solidarity?

J: We're a group. A school of thought. A style. Like the Bloomsbury Group or Provincetown or The Cedar Tavern. We can't break up over a little difference about "who stole/*influenced* who." Can we?

BRETT: Sure we can.

SASKIA: Yeah, I think so.

J: We're part of a generational wave. Writers of a time and place, of social complexity and cultural communality. If we dissolve, so much goes with us. Huh? Agreed?

BRETT: All right. Agreed. So?

J: Well…so…forgiven?

SASKIA: Forgiven? Well…well…all right. Forgiven.

J: Forgiven?

BRETT: Yeah, yeah, I forgive us, too.

J: And we're all friends again?

BRETT: Solidarity.

SASKIA: Solidarity.

(They all clink glasses.)

J: As artists, as writers, as leaders within our craft and community.

SASKIA: *(More chipper.)* Yes!

BRETT: Yes!

J: Yes! *(Drinks. Beat.)* Is it time?

BRETT: *(Glances at watch.)* Yes. I think it's time now.

J: *(Beginning to rise.)* As writers…

SASKIA: *(Rising.)* …artists…

BRETT: *(Sliding out of the booth.)* …and leaders.

J: *(Standing now.)* Yes.

(We now see that Brett and J are wearing aprons at their waists. They take up two trays. Saskia picks up two large menus from the table, turns down front, and, with a pearly smile, says:)

SASKIA: Good evening. Table for two?

(Blackout.)

END OF PLAY

Electric Roses
by David Howard

CHARACTERS
RUSS

SARA

DARRELL

SETTING
A bus station and a cell in a county jail.

Electric Roses

Scene: The scene reflects two different locations. The first is the waiting area of a bus station in Yuma, Arizona. Seated on a bench in this area is Sara. She has a suitcase sitting on the floor next to her. She wears slightly heavy make-up, which covers a few bruises on her face. The second area is a cell in a county jail, although it may be suggested by only a straight-backed chair. On the chair sits Russ, Sara's husband. The two never see one another. They exist together for the audience's convenience.

RUSS: *(For the most part, his tone throughout the play is fairly reflective. He addresses the audience directly.)* The day I married Sara it was so hot, you could'a fried an egg on the hood of my truck...musta been a hundred and five—hundred and six, maybe...Course, there's nothing special about that...it was June... It's funny how things can stick in your mind, isn't it? Three years ago, an' I can still almost feel it... Shit it was hot... So me an' Darrell was drinkin' beer... Guess there's nothing special 'bout that either...
(Darrell, Russ's best friend, appears in the other area. Sara sees him. There is a tense silence between them.)

SARA: ...Hello, Darrell.

DARRELL: *(Quietly.)* Hi.

SARA: ...What are you doing here?

DARRELL: Lookin' for you.

SARA: Why'd you come here?

DARRELL: Looked everywhere else...saw your truck.

SARA: It's not mine, it belongs to Russ...

DARRELL: Well...yeah.

RUSS: I guess I drink too much. I know that...I'd be lying if I didn't say it scared me sometimes. *(He thinks a moment.)* So, where was I?... Oh, yeah, it was hot, an' Darrell says, "Why don't we go to Vegas?" An' I said, "When?" An' he said, "Right now!" *(Sara sits back down.)*

DARRELL: I saw Russ, too.

SARA: When?

DARRELL: This morning.

SARA: Yeah?

DARRELL: Yeah. *(Pause.)*

SARA: How is he?

DARRELL: You haven't seen him?

SARA: No.

DARRELL: Umm…

SARA: *(Quietly.)* …didn't think it was such a good idea.

DARRELL: …yeah …he feels pretty bad.

SARA: *(Thoughtfully, sincerely.)* I know he does.

DARRELL: He'll be out by noon.

SARA: I'll be outta here by then.

RUSS: You ever been to Las Vegas?… It's something, I'll tell you… You gotta go at night, though. All those lights, shit, it's something. *(He laughs a little.)* Somebody said they musta built it at night, 'cause it's so damn ugly in the day. An' Darrell said the only thing you ought to do in Las Vegas is eat. You try to do anything else, they're just taking your money… Course, you can drink for nothing if you gamble, but… I suppose he's right anyhow…you can't drink enough to make it worthwhile. *(Sara takes out a cigarette.)*

SARA: You gotta match?

DARRELL: *(As he takes out some matches.)* Shouldn't do that, you know. It can kill you. *(She laughs as he lights her cigarette. As she laughs, she grimaces a little and holds her side.)*

SARA: Ohh…

DARRELL: You all right?

SARA: Yeah…just breathed in too much. *(She stops a moment, closes her eyes, and holds her side.)*

RUSS: So, we figured, you know, what the hell, you gotta do something, you can't just sit there…an' you know as well as I do there's nothing to do here in Yuma at night… Shit, the sun goes down, this place turns into a damn graveyard. Feel like you're in Tubac or somewhere.

SARA: You know, Darrell, if you hadn't been with him last night, I could be dead now. *(Darrell stands uncomfortably, not answering.)* You talk to Abby last night when you got home?

DARRELL: No, she was asleep.

RUSS: So, he called Abby, an' we went to get Sara. She was working. She works over at Jerry's Tastee Cone… Used to be the Tastee Freeze, till they run outta money. Now it's the Tastee Cone… An' we go over there, an' said, you know, we're goin' to Vegas. You wanna come?

SARA: Took me three minutes to get down the stairs this morning.

DARRELL: …You look good.

SARA: Yeah?

DARRELL: Yeah, you can hardly tell.

SARA: *(She smiles slightly.)* Thanks… I don't like to wear so much make-up.

DARRELL: I know…but, it looks okay…kinda sexy.

SARA: *(As she laughs.)* Darrell, you always were full of shit.

RUSS: An' she said, "I gotta change my clothes. I can't go to Las Vegas with hot fudge all over me." So we went to Darrell's and got Abby and then went over to pick up Sara…an' … *(He thinks a moment.)* When she came outta her place, she'd…fixed herself all up…see, she was good at that, real good… I can still see her in my head. *(He pauses again.)* I guess I will for the rest of my life.

DARRELL: So…where you headed? *(Sara shakes her head.)* Come on, Sara.

SARA: Darrell, if he figured you knew, he'd get it out of you one way or another.

DARRELL: …yeah, I suppose he would…north?

SARA: I guess.

DARRELL: …don't go to your sister's. That's the first place he'll go.

SARA: I'm not stupid, Darrell.

DARRELL: Yeah…sorry.

RUSS: You see, a woman like Sara… I mean, she was pretty an' all, but…that ain't it. It was like, when I looked at her, something happened… *(He puzzles over what he feels.)* She put a hook inside of me that wasn't ever gonna let go…I knew that…I knew that the minute it happened.

DARRELL: You need money or something?

SARA: No.

DARRELL: I can run over to the bank. Only take a minute.

SARA: No, I'm alright.

DARRELL: You sure?

SARA: I'm fine. *(Pause.)*

DARRELL: Well here. *(Takes $10 out of his wallet and hands it to her.)* Let me buy you lunch…wherever…

SARA: *(Resignedly.)* Thanks, Darrell. *(She takes the money.)*

RUSS: You know, I woke up this morning, an' my hand was busted…it was all wrapped up, an' it hurt like hell. *(He examines it a moment.)* An' I looked at it, and I thought, "What the hell's happened to you?" You know? Did that ever happen to you? You know, where you wake up, and there's something different, and you didn't even know it?

DARRELL: What are you gonna do?

SARA: I don't know. Get a job, I guess.

DARRELL: Well…you can always get a job in Vegas. It's easy to work there, I hear.

SARA: *(Looks at Darrell.)* …I'll keep it in mind.

DARRELL: You know, Sara… *(Not sure about continuing—he does anyway.)* …you're the best thing that ever happened to Russ. *(Pause.)* This is gonna kill him. You know that, don't you?

SARA: I can't think about that. *(Pause.)*

DARRELL: I just want to know if you're sure, that's all.

SARA: If I wasn't sure, I wouldn't be here.

DARRELL: *(Quietly.)* Yeah.

RUSS: So, anyway, we're driving up there. We're out there in the desert, up past Needles, an' you know, there ain't nothing out there. It's just black. An' Darrell pulls the car over, and, I don't know, runs off to take a piss or something, an' me and Sara get out of the car…. Abby was asleep. She always does that in the car… An' you know, there's nothing around… The only light you've got is from the stars. And I'm telling you, you look up and you look up and you can see things you never believed were up there…

SARA: *(Troubled.)* It's not just this, you know…not just…last night.

DARRELL: I know.

SARA: *(Begins to cry a little.)* Sometimes, it would scare me to go out of the house, the way he'd look… I felt I couldn't breathe, you know?

DARRELL: Sara, you don't have to tell me nothing. *(A pause. Sara looks at a diamond necklace which she wears around her neck.)*

SARA: You remember when he bought this? *(Darrell nods.)* In Vegas?

DARRELL: Yeah.

SARA: I remember, he took me outside to show it to me. And he held it in his hand up over my head. And I could see it glittering there in the dark… you couldn't see nothing but the light sparkling on it. And he said, "You know what that is, Sara?" And I said, "What?" An' he said, "That's you. That's what you are to me."

RUSS: We were standing there, an' I could feel her there next to me…that dark all around us. And I said, "You know why we're going to Vegas, don't you?" And she said, "Why's that?" And, I said, "So I can marry you." And she said, "Bullshit." An' I said, "I am. I'm takin' you to Vegas, and I'm gonna marry you when we get there." And she laughs, and she says, "Why in the hell should I marry you?" And I said… *(His tone become much more significant—the words mean considerably more.)* I said, " 'Cause no one in the world is ever gonna feel what I feel for you right now." *(There is a pause.)*

DARRELL: *(Frustrated.)* God damn it!… You know things would be a lot easier if you could just tell him to go to hell, you know?

SARA: Yeah…

DARRELL: Just tell him to go screw himself.

SARA: Yeah… *(Pause.)*

DARRELL: Not that easy though, is it?

RUSS: Hell, I don't know what was in her head to say yes to me, but she did. I guess maybe she knew how much I wanted it… *(He thinks a moment.)* First thing we did when we hit town was find a place that would do it for us. You know, they've got places that will do it all night. And we found one…this little white house with electric roses that lit up the outside, an'… I married her.

DARRELL: You know what Abby's gonna do to me when she finds out I was here, don't you? Hell, it might be better if I got on the bus with you. *(In spite of herself, Sara smiles. Mock seriousness.)* You know, you're ruining our social life, don't you? I mean, shit, who's Abby gonna play cards with?

SARA: She can call Cheryl Ann.

DARRELL: The hell she will. Cheryl Ann's not coming in my house. She's nothing but trash, cheap trash. *(Sara laughs.)* Well, she is.

RUSS: Later on, we were sitting in this bar… Darrell's eating shrimp cocktail. You know, forty-nine cents. An' Abby's over playing the nickel slots. An' this guy…this asshole keno player… He's got this shirt with flowers all over it, and his hair looks like…you know, Mr. California Dude. An' he's sittin' there looking at Sara…just staring at her, an' you know what I'm talkin' about…Shit, I wanted to break his greasy neck. An' I said, "What are you lookin' at, pal?" An' he says, "Do you own her?" An' I said, "Yeah, I do." And then I broke his fuckin' nose. *(Over a speaker, we hear the voice of the bus station announcer.)*

ANNOUNCER: Ladies and gentlemen, the Trailways bus for Blythe, Lake Havasu, Las Vegas, and all points north is now boarding outside the terminal. Would all passengers ticketed for this route please make your way to the boarding area.

RUSS: If you could'a seen what he was doing...what his eyes were doing ... *(He stops to think.)* What he wanted...shit, if he were here now, I'd break it again, looking at her like that. *(Sara stands, grabs her suitcase, and begins moving out to the bus.)*

SARA: *(As they look at one another.)* Well, I guess I better...

DARRELL: Yeah...

RUSS: See, you gotta understand, a woman like that, geez, if you could see how they are around her.

DARRELL: *(His voice stops her exit.)* Sara...?

SARA: Huh?

RUSS: I start thinking about that, and...something happens inside of me.

DARRELL: *(He speaks with a pain in his voice.)* Umm... *(He thinks a moment.)* I guess I'm just gonna miss you, that's all. *(She looks at him for a moment, then crosses to him, and embraces him. They are both near tears.)*

RUSS: *(It is painful for him to speak.)* I admit it... I've hit her... *(Pause. He looks over the audience.)* Well, what do you want me to say? I'm not proud of it... Sometimes, when I drink...all them looks... *(Quietly.)* Sometimes, you just wonder how strong a person is, you know? *(As Darrell and Sara part.)*

SARA: You take care, Darrell.

DARRELL: Yeah.

SARA: Tell Abby goodbye for me.

DARRELL: I will. *(Sara crosses to the exit. She turns back.)*

SARA: *(As she cries.)* I love him, you know that.

DARRELL: Yeah, I know.

(The lights begin to fade on the bus station; it becomes nearly a silhouette as Russ finishes.)

RUSS: God knows, I love her... She's the most important thing in the world to me...she knows that, too. No matter what happens, she knows it.

END OF PLAY

Median
by John Stinson

CHARACTERS

HAYS
DANNY
SCOTTY

Median

A thin grassy median strip dividing a highway. Danny, a boy in his twenties, sits on the grass, looking at the cars zooming by. He looks at his watch, then returns his gaze to the road. He looks again, spots something he recognizes, then looks away at a different part of the traffic. A blaring horn is heard, followed by another. Hays, a woman in her twenties, pitches onto the median, landing near Danny and puffing hysterically.

HAYS: What the hell are you doing out here?

DANNY: Waiting.

HAYS: Did you see me almost get mauled?

DANNY: Yeah. First one looked like a Beemer. You'd have gotten a lot of dough.

HAYS: I almost got killed.

DANNY: Then again, they might not give you any money. I think crossing a highway's illegal.

HAYS: I know it is. And I know why. It's incredibly stupid.

DANNY: Well, only you can judge that about yourself.

HAYS: How long have you been out here?

DANNY: Since rush hour. This morning. 8:40. I crossed on over to the middle ground. Speeds were like this. Fuckin-A-fast.

HAYS: This is, then, a suicide attempt of sorts?

DANNY: Am I dead?

HAYS: Doesn't look it.

DANNY: No suicide. You?

HAYS: Concern for a friend. Not suicide.

DANNY: The way you deal with onrushing traffic, I might not have known. You gotta pick your lane and keep constant speed. That way the terrified motorists can gauge how best to avoid smashing into you.

HAYS: I didn't quite consider their end in the whole situation.

DANNY: You gotta think beyond your own skin, Hays.

HAYS: Fuck you. And fuck this banter. Hi, Danny. What the hell are you doing out here?

DANNY: Waiting.

HAYS: For?

DANNY: Rush hour. So I can go home.

HAYS: You're crossing back over?

DANNY: Yep. I expect twenty minutes from now will be prime time. Though it's packing up pretty good already. What the hell are you doing out here?

HAYS: I've been looking for you all day. Managed to spot you out here. Was stupid enough to run over here since you wouldn't acknowledge my presence on the other side.

DANNY: Thought that was you waving and flapping your arms. But it's so hard to see past all these cars. I really wish they wouldn't put them in our way when we're trying to party.

HAYS: You are being an incredible jerk.

DANNY: Well, you were a moron to come out here. At least I've got a legit reason to be sitting here.

HAYS: And that is?

DANNY: I hate my petty problems. Dodging a roaring Buick makes me forget them. Plus, life's less boring.

HAYS: So this is some thrill-seeking expedition?

DANNY: Sure there's some thrill in it... You know, if I hadn't already made people think I'm a liberal, I'd join some war. That's perfect. I'd like to get in on some of that.

HAYS: I guess it's my job to convince you otherwise?

DANNY: I didn't force you to follow me out here.

HAYS: I came anyway.

DANNY: I know. And I think you should seek professional help. This could be indicative of a larger problem.

HAYS: I care about you.

DANNY: Believe it or not, I feel the same about you. Didn't expect you to go running into that shit, though.

HAYS: Neither did I.

DANNY: So why did you? People who care call the paramedics or Nurse Ratched or something. Why'd you take the leap of doom?

HAYS: You haven't finished telling me why for you.

DANNY: H-A-Y-S.

HAYS: I was worried I might be one of the reasons.

DANNY: Yeah?

HAYS: Yeah.

DANNY: Well, don't worry. It's just that I feel shitty.

HAYS: You don't have to feel that way.

DANNY: What way do you think I feel?

HAYS: If I had to guess?

DANNY: Yeah.

HAYS: Useless. You feel useless. To the universe.

DANNY: That's the problem with having friends, they get to know you inside and out.

HAYS: And that's what I mean. You don't have to feel that way. You've got friends. Friends who love you.

DANNY: Convince me that love will make me not feel this way.

HAYS: It's not that easy. Things take a little more sweat than that.

DANNY: Then I'd rather feel this way.

HAYS: Thanks. Thanks a lot, Danny. You grant me a whole lot of value with that one.

DANNY: I didn't mean it. But you know, we aren't even lovers.

HAYS: I can't love my best friend?

DANNY: Are you sure that's all?

HAYS: Yeah.

DANNY: Sure?

HAYS: Yeah, that's all.

DANNY: *(Getting up, walking toward road.)* Well, then I just better get back across that road. Wouldn't want to be upsetting my friend.

HAYS: Danny.

DANNY: No, no. I'm all right. Friends.

(Danny steps a little into traffic.)

HAYS: Okay, okay! I like you more than that. You big stupid asshole.

DANNY: Sorry. Sit out on a median all day, Hays, and you start to lose hope for humanity. Watching thousands of mechanized egos in full armor at ramming speed.

HAYS: Yeah, well, all those mechanized egos fly home, but when they walk into the apartment or whatever, the answering machine has two blinks going. That's two friends incredibly glad to hear that person's voice when she finally calls. You know? This is not because they're all doing it. It's because we give up those ridiculous egos and just breathe with each other and admit that it's pretty hard sometimes. But we make contact and we live outside ourselves a little.

DANNY: Man. I thought a soundtrack was going to kick in.

HAYS: I'm serious.

DANNY: I know. I'm just being an asshole.

HAYS: So what do you have for me?

DANNY: Okay, I guess I came out here hoping you'd get mad and give up on me. Then I'd have to chase you for a change. Maybe I'd actually do something.

HAYS: But I followed you, as always.

DANNY: Yeah, you did. Right to the fucking median.

HAYS: The only way to get me to give up on you is to treat me real bad.

DANNY: And I wouldn't treat you bad. Not real bad.

HAYS: You'd just treat you bad.

DANNY: Yeah.

HAYS: And you never see any link between those things?

DANNY: I guess not.

(Hays gets up and walks toward the edge of the highway. She jumps forward into a lane and leaps right back out.)

Cut it out! Cut it out!

HAYS: Get it?

DANNY: Yeah. A little. I get it a little.

HAYS: Look at me. Look at me every day.

(A loud horn is heard, followed by another. Scotty pitches onto the ground near Danny and Hays.)

SCOTTY: Hey. Hey you guys! Check this out, I made it across too. Could have been Ford Fodder. Could have been Mack Truck Meat. Could have been Jeep Juice. But I made it. Oh. Are you guys having a moment? I could just, you know, turn back around… *(Scotty faces the traffic again. Turns back around right away.)* No. That would be completely insane.

HAYS: Scott, come sit down over here.

SCOTTY: So what the hell are you doing here?

HAYS: I followed him.

SCOTTY: What the hell's he doing out here?

HAYS: It's as close as he could get to Bosnia.

SCOTTY: Turn on the TV, Danny-boy. You get plenty of Bosnia.

DANNY: Yeah. Well. What are you doing out here?

SCOTTY: Didn't want to miss out.

HAYS: On what?

SCOTTY: On whatever this is. You got to admit, seeing two people running around a median strip at rush hour—it's tempting. There has to be something up with that. So what are you guys doing here?

DANNY: Watching humanity suck.

HAYS: Nothing.

SCOTTY: Really?

HAYS: We were just hanging out.

SCOTTY: Oh. You're just…sitting?

HAYS: More or less.

DANNY: She chased me, Scotty. Couldn't help herself.

HAYS: I couldn't help that you act like this, and I have to come hold your hand.

DANNY: Hey, I was doing fine, and would have been home ten minutes from now, and you'd have never known.

SCOTTY: You guys want me to migrate down the median a bit?

DANNY: Nah. I was just kidding. I was all mopey and Hays came out to talk to me. It was very sweet of her.

HAYS: Thanks.

SCOTTY: You're surprised by this?

DANNY: I guess not. I guess I shouldn't be. That Hays, she's a real Samaritan.

HAYS: You know, I know about your wanting to chase me. That's why I never run. I know it messes with you. I love that. Part of why I let you get away with this stuff.

DANNY: Yeah?

HAYS: Yeah.

(Danny looks at Hays for a second, looks again to the road, and leaps up and out into the traffic. Hays turns her head and the honking blares.)

SCOTTY: Jesus, Dan! Dan! Back in the war zone. *(Pause.)* He made it. Barely.

HAYS: I don't care.

SCOTTY: You want to go after him?

HAYS: No. No, I don't. I won't. *(Scotty pulls out a pack of cigarettes and offers one to Hays. She shakes her head no. He pulls the pack back, then immediately offers it again. Hays takes the cigarette.)* Thanks.

SCOTTY: Hays? Do you like him?

HAYS: I don't think I get to.

SCOTTY: Yep. You want to stay here? You're sure?

HAYS: Not about much.

SCOTTY: It's safer here.

HAYS: Yeah. It is.

END OF PLAY

Cover
by Jeffrey Sweet
with Stephen Johnson and Sandra Hastie

CHARACTERS

MARTY

FRANK

DIANE

SETTING

An office.

Cover

At rise: An office. Frank is working at his desk. Marty enters.

MARTY: Work, work, work.

FRANK: Oh, Marty.

MARTY: I'm early.

FRANK: You're early.

MARTY: If I'm interrupting…

FRANK: No, this is nothing. Just odds and ends.

MARTY: Nice office.

FRANK: Oh, that's right—you've never been up here, have you?

MARTY: No, this is the first time.

FRANK: Well, you've got to take a look out this window. I've got a view that will knock your eyes out. My big status symbol.

MARTY: You've got to be good, they give you a window like this. They've got to like you.

FRANK: See Jersey over there?

MARTY: I'll be damned, Jersey.

FRANK: What's great is to watch thunderstorms come over the Hudson. Hell of a show. Lightning and huge gothic clouds.

MARTY: Always said that was the best thing that could happen to New Jersey.

FRANK: Well, OK.

MARTY: No, I'm impressed. I really am. This is very nice.

FRANK: Yes, I'm very…

MARTY: So, you all set and ready to go?

FRANK: Just let me put this stuff away.

MARTY: Take your time.

FRANK: Where's Diane?

MARTY: Oh, she'll be along in a few minutes. I told her to meet me here. She had an appointment crosstown, so I figured…

FRANK: Sure.

MARTY: Actually, I'm glad I got here a little earlier. There's a favor I want to ask of you.

FRANK: Ask away.

MARTY: OK. Well, see, as a topic of conversation, it may come up during the evening where I was last night. And it would make it a lot easier if we could decide between us that I was with you.

FRANK: To say that?

MARTY: Not to say necessarily, but to sort of give the impression that we were together. It would make things a lot simpler for me. I mean, if it comes up.

FRANK: You want me to say…

MARTY: Just to say…

FRANK: That you and I…

MARTY: That we were…

FRANK: Together…

MARTY: Together…

FRANK: Last night.

MARTY: Yeah.

FRANK: You want me to lie.

MARTY: Well…

FRANK: Not "well." You want me to lie.

MARTY: Well…

FRANK: That's what you're asking.

MARTY: I wouldn't put it…

FRANK: Is that what you're asking?

MARTY: Well, yes.

FRANK: To lie?

MARTY: A little bit. Just to give the impression so that Diane won't worry. To avoid confusion and upset for her.

FRANK: I see. You want me to do a favor for you for her.

MARTY: I couldn't have said it better myself.

FRANK: Where were you last night? I mean, I have to know.

MARTY: It doesn't matter.

FRANK: Well, yes, it does. I have to know whether you're wanting me to tell a white lie or a black lie.

MARTY: It's a white lie.

FRANK: How white? I mean, where were you?

MARTY: I was out.

FRANK: Alone? With someone?

MARTY: With someone.

FRANK: Yeah?

MARTY: Diane wouldn't understand.

FRANK: A woman?

MARTY: She'd take it the wrong way.

FRANK: You were out with another woman.

MARTY: Yes, I was out with another woman.

FRANK: I see. And that's a white lie?

MARTY: It's no big deal.

FRANK: I'm sorry, I can't do it.

MARTY: Hey, really, it's no big deal.

FRANK: No, I wouldn't feel good about it.

MARTY: Why not? It's just a little favor.

FRANK: It's not a little… You're asking me to lie to her. You don't understand. She's my friend.

MARTY: Aren't I your friend?

FRANK: You're my friend and she's my friend. But she's not my friend because you're my friend. I mean, it's not that you and I have a primary friendship and she's a secondary friend by extension. You're both primary friends.

MARTY: I understand that.

FRANK: You don't break that trust.

MARTY: I'm not asking you to break that trust. I'm asking you to spare her confusion and upset.

FRANK: You're asking me to lie to her.

MARTY: To give a different impression of the truth.

FRANK: A false impression, which is a lie.

MARTY: You've never told a lie in your life?

FRANK: That's not the issue.

MARTY: Of course it's the issue. You're saying you don't tell lies.

FRANK: I'm saying I will not tell this lie.

MARTY: How do you decide when you will or will not tell a lie?

FRANK: I try not to lie.

MARTY: But what makes you decide if you'll tell a given lie? Say that an opportunity for a lie presents itself—how do you decide if you'll tell it?

FRANK: This is not the issue.

MARTY: You have told lies, haven't you? You've told lies in the past.

FRANK: I have, but that has nothing to do with this.

MARTY: You just won't tell a lie for me.

FRANK: I don't want to tell an active lie, no.

MARTY: Well, are you going to tell her that I was out with another woman last night?

FRANK: No, of course not.

MARTY: Then isn't that creating a false impression? Isn't that, in fact, a lie?

FRANK: That's a passive lie, my not telling something.

MARTY: Ah, that's different.

FRANK: It is.

MARTY: A difference in kind, right? Active versus passive.

FRANK: There *is* a difference, whether you see it or not.

MARTY: Would you care to elaborate?

FRANK: What do you mean?

MARTY: On the distinction. Active, passive.

FRANK: What does this have to do with…?

MARTY: If we correlate an active lie as being a lie you won't tell and a passive lie as a lie you will, then perhaps we can find that point in the gray area between where we can come to an understanding.

FRANK: Look, I don't want to lie to her.

MARTY: I'm not asking you to *want* to.

FRANK: You're just asking me to do it.

MARTY: Yes, as a favor to a friend.

FRANK: No, I don't want to.

MARTY: You do lots of things you don't want to do. Everybody does.

FRANK: The things that I sometimes do that I don't want to do are things that I have to do. I don't have to do this. I don't have to break that trust.

MARTY: No, and we don't have to be friends, either.

FRANK: Oh, come on. Are you saying if I won't lie for you we won't be friends anymore?

MARTY: Of course not. I'm just asking you for a favor.

FRANK: I can't do it.

MARTY: Can't means won't.

FRANK: Can't means can't.

MARTY: Can't means won't.

FRANK: Can't means can't.

MARTY: No, you could.

FRANK: I couldn't.

MARTY: You *could.*

FRANK: I couldn't.

MARTY: Your mouth could say the words. Physically, your mouth could say the words.

FRANK: I couldn't do it.

MARTY: Of course you could.

FRANK: No, I couldn't.

MARTY: You could, but what you're saying is you won't.

FRANK: I'm saying I can't.

MARTY: You're saying you won't.

FRANK: I'm saying... OK, I'm saying I won't because I can't.

MARTY: But you *could*.

FRANK: I wouldn't if I could, but I can't so I won't. Anyway, you don't want me to lie for you.

MARTY: Yes, I do.

FRANK: I'm a terrible liar. She'd see right through me.

MARTY: How do you know until you try?

FRANK: Look, I'm not going to tell her where you were. I mean, I couldn't because I don't know.

MARTY: I was at Marvin Gardens. That's on the West Side.

FRANK: I don't want to know. Don't tell me any more.

MARTY: Barbara Schaeffer.

FRANK: I don't want to know who.

MARTY: Barbara Schaeffer.

FRANK: Barbara Schaeffer?

MARTY: See, now you know.

FRANK: I wish you hadn't told me.

MARTY: But you know, and if you don't tell Diane that means you've already lied. Passive-shmassive, it's a lie, and if you've gone that far, why not go a little further for a friend?

FRANK: Look, you can argue rings around me, but I'm not going to.

MARTY: OK, sorry I asked.

FRANK: I wish you'd understand.

MARTY: It really is a hell of a nice office. You should be very proud. *(A beat. Diane enters.)*

DIANE: I've found you at last.

FRANK: You have trouble?

DIANE: You could've left a trail of breadcrumbs. So, you guys ready to go?

FRANK: In a second.

DIANE: Hey, nice view.

FRANK: You like it?

DIANE: That's Jersey, isn't it?

MARTY: You can see thunderstorms, Frank says.

DIANE: Oh really? That must be exciting.

FRANK: What, I don't get a kiss?

DIANE: Absolutely! *(She kisses Frank.)*

FRANK: Hey, you look swell.

DIANE: In contrast to…?

FRANK: No, of course not.

DIANE: Thank you.

FRANK: That's a nice outfit.

DIANE: I'm glad you like it.

FRANK: It really is. I really do. *(Frank goes offstage with a file.)*

DIANE: *(To Marty.)* So, how was your day?

MARTY: Fine.

DIANE: You and Jacobs get that thing cleared up?

MARTY: No big problem.

DIANE: I thought you were worried.

MARTY: Not seriously. We sat down, we talked.

DIANE: You compromised.

MARTY: I didn't have to.

DIANE: It must be a relief.

MARTY: And your interview?

DIANE: Nothing definite.

MARTY: But there's interest?

DIANE: They didn't say no.

MARTY: That's half the battle.

DIANE: Yeah.

MARTY: Fingers crossed. *(Frank returns.)*

DIANE: You got here early, hunh?

MARTY: Just a few minutes ago.

DIANE: You've got a lot of papers on your desk, Frank. You must work awfully hard.

FRANK: It just looks that way. Gives the impression I'm earning my money, which, of course, I'm not.

DIANE: Oh, no, I know you. Industrious. Kind, loyal, honest, brave. You're the only person I know who lives up to…what is it?

MARTY: *(A little dig.)* The Boy Scout code.

DIANE: *(An immediate echo.)* The Boy Scout code.

FRANK: I wouldn't know. I wasn't a Scout.

DIANE: I can see you loaded down with merit badges.

FRANK: Yes, well now, *Touch of Evil* starts at 7:10 at the museum, so that means we should figure out what restaurant in the area...

MARTY: We should be pushing along, right.

FRANK: There's not a big hurry, but if we want to have a few drinks first...

DIANE: *(To Marty.)* Hey...

MARTY: How are ya?

DIANE: What are you doing?

MARTY: Just saying hi to you. *(A beat.)*

DIANE: We have to be at the museum at what?

FRANK: Well, by seven at least.

DIANE: So, where shall we eat?

FRANK: How does Italian sound, or are you on a diet and don't want that, or what? Chinese?

DIANE: Do you think I should be on a diet?

FRANK: Women always seem to be on diets. Men, too. People in general.

DIANE: Women aren't always on diets. Some women diet. The heavy variety. They tend to diet.

FRANK: I can remember you being on some pretty screwy diets.

DIANE: You think I'm screwy?

FRANK: No, of course not. I didn't say that.

DIANE: I'm sorry. I'm a little weird tonight. The ozone or something.

FRANK: Sure, I mean, air quality does...

DIANE: *(Interrupting. To Marty.)* You didn't get home till really late last night.

MARTY: I know.

DIANE: I wasn't even awake when you got home.

MARTY: I know. I didn't want to disturb you.

DIANE: Listen to the man! My favorite thing in the world is to wrap my arms around him in bed and he says he doesn't want to disturb me. And you got up and left early this morning, too.

MARTY: I know. I had to get out.

DIANE: Away from me?

MARTY: No, no, of course not. I just had to leave.

DIANE: Why?

MARTY: I had someplace to be.

DIANE: Oh.

MARTY: Preparing for the Jacobs thing, you know.

DIANE: Yeah.

FRANK: Do you want me to leave? Would you rather be alone or…?

DIANE: *(Interrupting.)* I promised myself I wasn't going to ask this question. I mean, I was in the bathroom and I combed my hair and I looked in the mirror and I said to myself, "You're looking good, Diane. You're looking very good."

FRANK: You look terrific.

DIANE: *(Quiet, intense.)* Where were you last night? Where were you till so late?

MARTY: *(A beat, then—)* I was with Frank all night long. Isn't that right, Frank? *(A beat.)*

FRANK: Yeah, that's right. He was. With me. We were…

DIANE: With Frank?

MARTY: Yes. Is that what you were so worried about?

DIANE: Yes, I'm sorry. It's stupid.

FRANK: We were playing…

MARTY: Playing…

FRANK: Poker.

MARTY: Cards. I didn't want to tell you because, well, I know you don't like me gambling.

DIANE: No.

MARTY: And I lost a little last night.

FRANK: Yeah, I zapped him for a little.

DIANE: How much?

FRANK: Forty-something. He made me promise not to tell.

DIANE: I see. Well…

FRANK: Tell you what, dinner's on me tonight, OK?

DIANE: *(She knows they've been lying now. She looks at Frank very directly and says—)* Why not? *(A beat.)*

MARTY: I guess we better get going, hunh?

(Diane nods. She exits first. Frank and Marty exchange a look before exiting. Lights fade out.)

END OF PLAY

Plays
for
Two Women and One Man

Dancing with a Devil
by Brooke Berman

CHARACTERS

WOMAN

YOUNGER WOMAN

MAN

PLACE
Here.

TIME
Now.

Dancing with a Devil

A Woman is on the stage. A Younger Woman, the younger version of herself, is with her. The first Woman talks to the audience. A Man in a black turtleneck and black pants listens.

WOMAN: This is how it happens. I will tell it in the present tense so that you can be there with me. I will tell it in the present tense as if there were a way to reverse the story, to change the ending, so we can all hope together that it will be different.

YOUNGER WOMAN: I hate it when you tell it. It makes me feel afraid.

WOMAN: I am twenty-four years old and I live in New York City.

YOUNGER WOMAN: I really hate when you tell it. But I like the part before it happens. I like being young in New York.

I am twenty-four years old, and I live in New York City. My life is shiny and new and just barely discovered. I am an emerging something or other, waiting tables and writing stories. I go to parties with people whose skin sparkles and whose names are known. I like to tell stories about how I am twenty-four and still a virgin, deconstructing the relationship between my heart and my skin and my sex.

WOMAN: I was a virgin.

YOUNGER WOMAN: I like to dance, to feel air inside my body. I think that dancing will save me from pain. The music will earth me and the beat will bring me to the ground. I go dancing in gay bars with funny names. I take great pleasure being a girl in a boy bar, enjoying the fact that no one will try to pick me up. My life is safe. I play outrageous, but my life is safe. I have made it that way. Just enough outrage and lots of safety nets.

I live in an old apartment building in Soho, where the artists are, across the hall from a Mafia widow and next door to an idiot with a loud dog. I listen to the dog howl whenever he is alone. The sound of this drives me crazy, and I complain about it but the owner does not listen.

On the first day of the new year, I write down a list of my dreams and goals. I have many dreams—the foremost of which is this: "I want to be transformed." I write it down, "I want to be transformed," because that is what I want.

I look for my transformation anywhere I can. I look for it in the eyes of other people, but do not see it there. I look for it in the mountains of New Mexico, in the water of the hot springs, in the air of New York City and in the words that come to me while I dream. I dream that I am leaving an old city and moving to a new one and going to film school and leaving my mother.

It is June, and I am twenty-four, and I am about to be transformed.

WOMAN: It is June, June ninth to be precise, just barely after midnight, and I am about to fall asleep in my safe bed, in my safe Soho fourth-floor walk-up.

It is four in the morning and I open my eyes, certain that Sarah, my old roommate, has come home, though she moved out months ago and this makes no sense, I am sure that Sarah is in the apartment and I open my eyes, fully believing that I will see her there.

But I don't see Sarah. I see someone I do not know. I open my eyes to a stranger standing at the foot of my bed wearing a little black half-mask and a black turtleneck, looking a little bit like Zorro or like an existentialist Lone Ranger and I cannot understand how this stranger has penetrated my sleep or entered my apartment.

YOUNGER WOMAN: I don't like this part.

WOMAN: The stranger just stares at me. He doesn't move. He says, "Good evening."

MAN: Good evening.

WOMAN: And I say, Don't hurt me.

YOUNGER WOMAN: Don't hurt me.

WOMAN: And the stranger moves toward me, very very slowly like in slow motion, and I understand everything that is about to happen. I understand it in my mind before he even touches me. I think, this can't happen to me. I think, this can't happen to me because I am very smart. I have read Roland Barthes, and I know how to deconstruct sexuality. I am a virgin, and I am very smart, and things like this are not supposed to happen to people like me.

YOUNGER WOMAN: I really don't like this part.

MAN: I won't hurt you.

(The Younger Woman and the Man start to dance—a very slow ballroom dance. They dance throughout the next beat.)

WOMAN: He shows me the knife by running it across my ass so that I will feel that it is sharp and yet it leaves no mark. He leaves no mark. I will be taken to the hospital within an hour but there will be no mark that anything has happened to me.

YOUNGER WOMAN: But it is the present and I am not at the hospital yet. I am dancing with the devil right now in time that lasts longer than ordinary time. I say, "Please don't hurt me," and no one talks after that.

MAN: I won't hurt you.

YOUNGER WOMAN: I'm a virgin. I'm like the Virgin Mary. This can't happen to the Virgin Mary. And I think, you knew all along that this would happen to you. Who else were you saving yourself for?

MAN: You were saving yourself for me.

WOMAN: Maybe I was. How could I have known?

MAN: Everything will change now. Everything about you will change. You will no longer be who you were. You will have to become someone else to even understand this, to even put it behind you. You will leave your friends, your home, your family, in order to become the person who can put this behind herself. I am the answer to your prayers. I am giving you what you asked for. I am giving you the gift of transformation.

YOUNGER WOMAN: But I don't want to transform. Not like this. I don't want to go through with it.

MAN: You have no choice. You can fight me, or you can live.

WOMAN: I am light, and light I shall remain. That is what I was told to say.

YOUNGER WOMAN: I am light, and light I shall remain. I am in a time and place in which this event is not occurring. I am not in my body, and so you cannot touch me. You are filling me with your pain, with your body, but you are not touching me. You are not even near me, you are nowhere near me. I am held in the arms of angels and I am light, and light I shall remain.

(The Man and the Younger Woman stop dancing. The Man bows to the Woman and leaves the stage.)

WOMAN: It was over quickly. It seemed to take a long time, but I know that in the reality we will call reality, it happened within the span of ten, maybe fifteen minutes. He turned me over like some object and covered my head with a pillow and stuck his pain and his rage and his dick all inside me, and then it was over, and he was gone, as quietly and mysteriously as he came. He came out of the night and went back inside of it and was never caught.

YOUNGER WOMAN: He disappears. He is never caught. I run through the halls of my apartment building half naked looking for help.

WOMAN: I do not want to see women get raped anymore. Not in the movies, not in the theater, not on TV, and not in my bedroom. I do not want this experience. I do not want to see it and I do not want to relive it.

YOUNGER WOMAN: I am light and light I shall remain.

WOMAN: That's what the spirit guides told me to say. I am light, and light I shall remain. I cannot be hurt. But I was hurt.

I have taken the pain of some man that I do not know inside of me. I have taken it inside and transformed it, inside. I have gone to rape crisis centers and to therapy and to psychic healings in order to transform the pain that you stuck inside me one morning, me a stranger. I carry energy inside of me, some of which you deposited there, and rapists do not use condoms.

But I am not a repository for some stranger's suffering. Do you hear me? I DON'T WANT YOUR SUFFERING. YOU CAN JUST PUT IT SOMEWHERE ELSE. AND I HOPE THAT YOU SUFFER TILL THE END OF TIME, TILL THE END OF EVERYTHING, MAY YOUR SOUL KNOW WHAT YOU HAVE DONE TO ME AND MAY YOU BE…May you be healed.

YOUNGER WOMAN: I want to go home now.

WOMAN: We're almost done. We're almost at the end.

YOUNGER WOMAN: I'm hurt, and I want to go home.

WOMAN: I am going to tell it again.

YOUNGER WOMAN: Everything will change, he said. And it did. I did. Please don't tell it. I don't want to remember.

WOMAN: Everything will change, he said. Although he didn't really speak at all.

(The Man reappears.)

MAN: Good evening…

YOUNGER WOMAN: I want to go home now.

WOMAN: I am not twenty-four years old anymore. I do not know the people I knew then. My friends are different. My work is different. I have lived in seven different apartments in the span of three years. Everything has changed. I have changed.

YOUNGER WOMAN: Except that I still wake up at four in the morning expecting to find him there.

(The Man moves toward her.)

MAN: You are one of the statistics. You are about to become a statistic. One of the numbers. How many women in ten?

YOUNGER WOMAN: I don't want to dance with you.

WOMAN: I'm not going to tell it again.

YOUNGER WOMAN: I just want to go home.

WOMAN: I am twenty-eight years old, and I still live in New York. I sleep with a night light. I do not live alone. I stay at other people's houses when my roommates are away. I do not watch movies in which women are tracked, killed, hurt, maimed, terrorized, or raped. This means I do not watch a lot of movies. I meet young women who remind me of myself before it happened, and they scare me. I am afraid that something might happen to them too that will cause them to leave a piece of themselves behind forever. I hope this is not the case. I wish them well.

END OF PLAY

Under Lubianka Square
by Constance Congdon

CHARACTERS

RAYA TABACHNIKOFF: Age forty-plus, intelligent, well-educated, impoverished and desperate. Not Russian, from the Baltic States.

JENNIFER: Age twenty-five, a young, female American student. Nice, clueless.

MAN: A Mafia don, Russian-style.

PLACE

The metro station under Lubianka Square, near the Metropole Hotel, near Theatrical Square, Moscow.

TIME

1997.

Under Lubianka Square

A forty-plus-year-old woman runs into the space. She is dressed neatly but in out-of-style clothes, like from the seventies. She's carrying a beat-up gym bag with some inane slogan on it. This is Raya. She's pursued by Jennifer, an American student in her late twenties. Jennifer is dressed stylishly casual, a little showily, in fact, and carries a camera bag. Raya has a Russian accent.

RAYA: Are you crazy? Are you crazy?

JENNIFER: No.

RAYA: You act like a crazy person!

JENNIFER: *(Approaching her.)* I—

RAYA: Get away from me!

JENNIFER: Calm down. Someone—

RAYA: I hope. I hope they come arrest you.

JENNIFER: No! Stop it! Don't talk like that! Someone might *hear* you. Look—

RAYA: You are a bad person.

JENNIFER: I am not! I—I'm a student.

RAYA: Students can be bad. Students can be the worst.

JENNIFER: But I'm not. The worst. I'm just an American girl—woman.

RAYA: "Girl-woman"? What is that? Some TV talk from Los Angeles?

JENNIFER: You know Los Angeles?

RAYA: I'm not ignorant!

JENNIFER: I know that. I just wondered if you'd been there.

RAYA: I don't have money to travel.

JENNIFER: I'm sorry. Look, I'm sorry about everything. I'm sorry about the *whole fucking world!* I just wanted to take your picture. I mean, it was just a neat picture. You and all those women lined up, holding up those different jars and things—

RAYA: We are selling toiletries in the subway for money. That is "neat" to you.

JENNIFER: Well, *yeah*. I mean, it's social change and everything!

RAYA: What can you be thinking of—trying to take my picture! I am humiliated by what I have to do. You are the most rude American I have ever met.

JENNIFER: Canadian—I'm a Canadian.

RAYA: Say "house."

JENNIFER: *(American accent.)* House.

RAYA: Say "about."

JENNIFER: *(Faking a Canadian accent.)* Aboot.

RAYA: Too late. Why do you deny your country?

JENNIFER: I'm embarrassed about it. Particularly when people, like yourself, get mad at me for reasons I don't understand.

RAYA: You should get down on your knees and thank God every day you are an American.

JENNIFER: You sound like my father. Isn't that funny? He will be, like, so amazed to hear that some Russian woman—

RAYA: I am *not* Russian! I am from the Baltic.

JENNIFER: But this is *Russia*. Why be here…then?

(Raya pauses to try to take in Jennifer's complete lack of knowledge.)

RAYA: When history was taught you, you were napping? Drawing pictures of Elvis on your notebook, perhaps?

JENNIFER: Elvis? Hardly. He was disgusting. Why people liked him, I don't know. He was fat.

RAYA: Nichevo. Never mind. I'm going.

JENNIFER: Wait. I feel bad. Let me buy something. What's that?

RAYA: Hairspray.

JENNIFER: I'll buy that.

RAYA: Dollars.

JENNIFER: I have some Finmarks, some centimes, rubles—

RAYA: No rubles. No dollars? Finmarks, then.

JENNIFER: Wait. Here's a dollar.

(Raya sees inside Jennifer's purse.)

RAYA: What's that? Cigarettes?

JENNIFER: Merits.

RAYA: No L&Ms? Camels? Marlboro hard pack?

JENNIFER: Those will kill you. L&Ms? Who smokes L&Ms?

RAYA: My son.

JENNIFER: Okay. Here's a dollar.

RAYA: I need more.

JENNIFER: It's a little can of hairspray.

RAYA: Do you know how much this would cost you at GUM?

JENNIFER: What is GUM? Oh, that terrible mall.

RAYA: It is wonderful. For years it smelled of urine and had no merchandise except some pathetic Russian-made goods.

JENNIFER: It still smells of urine.

RAYA: It does NOT! It has a BODY SHOP! You can buy French mousse for your hair—Yves Rouchet—excellent brands like that!

JENNIFER: All right. If you say so.

RAYA: You can buy anything in Moscow now!

JENNIFER: If that's so, why are you dressed like that?

RAYA: Because you silly, vapid American baby cow, I HAVE NO MONEY!! Why do you think I'm selling hairspray in the subway??

JENNIFER: Your English is very good.

RAYA: So is my French, my German, and my Czech. Sprechen zie Deutsch? Parlez vous Français? *(In French.)* Peut-être tu serais plus gentille si tu parles français. (Perhaps you would be nicer if you spoke French.)

JENNIFER: I'm sorry. I only speak English.

RAYA: I must have three dollars for the hairspray. Unless you have some condoms.

JENNIFER: Wait. I have—

(Jennifer digs in her purse, finds something.)

RAYA: This is—what is this?

JENNIFER: It's a condom. "In case of emergency, break plastic and save a life."

RAYA: It's a toy.

JENNIFER: It's a keychain. From GMHC. Gay Men's Health Crisis. Keep it.

RAYA: I don't need a keychain. I need a condom.

JENNIFER: HERE.

(Jennifer hands her all the money of various kinds.)

RAYA: *(Hands Jennifer the hairspray.)* Here.

JENNIFER: Wait.

RAYA: No exchanges. No refunds.

JENNIFER: WAIT! I can't use this.

RAYA: Why not?

JENNIFER: Fluorocarbons. It has fluorocarbons.

RAYA: And this is important? Why?

JENNIFER: Fluorocarbons are bad.

RAYA: Life is bad.

JENNIFER: No, I mean it. This stuff is very bad. I can't—I won't use it.

RAYA: Then SELL IT TO SOMEONE!

JENNIFER: Look—I have some standards! And the environment is one of them. This hairspray is evil.

RAYA: Look, Minnie Mouse, many things are evil. Stalin was evil. Hitler was evil, only not as evil as Stalin.

JENNIFER: Stalin was more evil than Hitler? Oh, I don't think so—

RAYA: You don't think? Twenty million people *dead*. Entire cultures—songs, history, language, people—*swept off the face of the earth* by his withered arm. People we never knew and never will know. So he is the tyrant of the twentieth century. Think of all the other centuries and the buried towns, destroyed down to their fragments. You pick up a rock with some marking on it, think it's Greek—maybe it's part of a story stone from some hill people who called themselves by a name we will never hear. Spoke a language we will never hear. Knew secrets we will never discover. That is evil. Hairspray is not evil.

JENNIFER: But there's a hole in the ozone.

RAYA: A what in the what?

JENNIFER: Above Antarctica. A big hole. They've photographed it.

RAYA: People are starving and your country is spending money taking pictures of a hole above a continent where no one could live???

JENNIFER: But it affects all of us! We need the ozone layer because it protects us from the UV rays of the sun.

RAYA: So fat ladies in Miami don't get skin cancer?

JENNIFER: How can you know so much and not know this important fact?

RAYA: What "fact"? What are you talking about? You are a child! The fact is I have an advanced degree in classical and Biblical literature from Moscow University. I was translating Biblical literature from the Greek just seven years ago. The fact is I am unemployed and have to take care of my husband who has heart pain every night. The fact is my grandchild is sickly and we have to make his baby food from bad ingredients because we can't buy good vegetables and meat. The facts are that seven of us are living in two rooms and we are educated, civilized people! With sensibility and pride and an unfortunately highly developed inability to lie to ourselves! We wash out condoms so we can have sex without getting pregnant. Because we can't pay for birth control pills. And because I have already had eight abortions in my life and my daughter-in-law has had three and we still can conceive, in spite of all the scraping and damage. Now those are the facts!

JENNIFER: You know you just may be too hostile to sell anything to anyone. Have you thought about that? I mean, people don't like to be yelled at. In my opinion, there's too much yelling in the world. I turn on the TV and there are people yelling at each other and at the cameras and I ask, Jennifer, what are they all so angry about? I mean, everyone has problems! I, myself, have problems.

RAYA: What problems do you have?

JENNIFER: Well—thanks for asking—I, right now, have to pee and don't know where there's a bathroom. *And*, I'm not through, so don't give me that look. *And*, I—

(A large Russian man, in a slick-surfaced suit, very Eurotrash/Mafia don, enters and stares at Raya. He is suave, warm, and gracious to Jennifer and threatening to Raya.)

MAN: *(To Jennifer.)* Priviet.

JENNIFER: "Private"? No, we're not private. I don't know her, actually—we just met—are you a…policeman?

(Man laughs a lot at this.)

JENNIFER: What's so funny?

RAYA: He said hello, that's all. "Priviet" means hello.

JENNIFER: Wait. I can say a couple of things. *(To Man.)* Do-bro Oo-tra.

MAN: *(Very gracious.)* Good evening—viecher. Dobry viecher, young lady.

JENNIFER: *(Titillated.)* Oh. Thanks. *(Sudden realization.)* Gosh, is it evening? I'm supposed to meet my friends at my hotel—I don't even know where I am.

MAN: Metropole Hotel is that way.

JENNIFER: Thanks. How did you know which hotel I was staying at?

MAN: I had a lucky guess.

JENNIFER: Well, I should be going. *(Hands Raya back the hairspray.)* Keep this. And the money.

MAN: *(To Raya, in Russian.)* Ty opiat'u metro torguesh? I mne nichego ne otstiogiuaesh Plati, ato skvartiroi rasproshshaeshsia! (You were selling in the subway again? YOU BETTER PAY ME MY SHARE OR YOU WILL LOSE YOUR FLAT! Do you understand?)

JENNIFER: Do you know each other?

MAN: Yes, we're old friends.

JENNIFER: I figured as much. I thought maybe you were her husband.

MAN: No. Her husband is a small man.

JENNIFER: With a heart condition.

MAN: Yes, he has a weak, weak heart. From too much worry. It's very bother-some—change. Change is very hard to live through. Many, many didn't live through it. And many more will not, also.

RAYA: *(About the eternality of Mafia/KGB/thug power.)* We're married. Since time began. And we will never, never be separated, it seems.

JENNIFER: Oh, then you are married. I thought you said he was sick, your hus-band. *(To Man.)* You don't look sick. You look really, really healthy.

MAN: Thank you for the compliment. I try to keep in shape. I eat well. I eat very well, in fact. For lunch, I had a chimichanga at La Kantina on Tverskaya Street. It cost twelve American dollars. It had meat, lots of it, cheese, pouring out of it. And five small tomatoes—fresh and good. Then I had apple pie, deep-dish American apple pie with ice cream on it for pudding. I mean, dessert. And I drank two glasses of milk. And a Coke.

RAYA: He is not my husband.

JENNIFER: But—

MAN: Raya means that we are married another way. Don't you, Mrs. Tabachnikoff?

RAYA: Yes.

JENNIFER: How? I don't understand.

RAYA: You should have stayed awake in history, detochka. It's already made your country and you can't see it.

JENNIFER: What? What are you two talking about? You're speaking English, but I can't understand what you're talking about!

RAYA: You will never grow up! You will lose your country because you refuse to grow up! Become educated!

JENNIFER: Why? It hasn't done you any good, has it? I mean, has it? You're selling shit in the subway. And yelling at tourists. You have no baby food! No heart medicine! condoms! What has your education gotten you? History? I HATE FUCKING HISTORY! IT'S FUCKING BORING! IT HAS NOTHING TO DO WITH ME! WE STARTED OVER! DO YOU HEAR ME? WE STARTED OVER! WITH OUR OWN RULES!! I'M AN AMERICAN! AND I AM FINE! LOOK AT THESE CLOTHES! LOOK AT THIS HAIRCUT! THIS CAMERA BAG! I EAT WELL! I SLEEP WELL! *(Jennifer begins pummeling Raya with her camera bag.)* I'M GODDAM FUCKING HAPPY!!! HAPPY, DO YOU HEAR ME!!! HAPPY!!!!!

MAN: *(Getting Jennifer off Raya.)* Wait! Wait! Stop now! *(Taking camera bag.)* This is heavy.

JENNIFER: Oh god. I forgot that had my camera in it. Is it okay? Is she okay?

MAN: She's fine.

JENNIFER: Are—are you okay?

RAYA: I'm fine.

JENNIFER: I'm really sorry. I—I never do that! I swear!

RAYA: I'm fine.

JENNIFER: I've never hit anyone—ever…before.

RAYA: Perhaps you never had a good enough reason.

JENNIFER: I was brought up better than this.

(But to Raya "this" means the subway and the way she has to live.)

RAYA: That is obvious.

JENNIFER: I'm a good person.

RAYA: So am I.

(Jennifer gets some money from some place where she's hidden it—her bra or her shoe.)

JENNIFER: Here is all my money—that I'm carrying.

MAN: No, no, she doesn't need it. Her son will drink it up.

JENNIFER: I thought he only smoked.

RAYA: He does whatever he can.

(Man folds the money back into Jennifer's hand.)

MAN: Don't encourage her. Allow me to walk you to your hotel.

JENNIFER: Thank you. Spah-see-bah.

MAN: Pahzhaloostah, my dear.

(He starts to lead Jennifer off, but Jennifer is compelled to finish something with Raya.)

JENNIFER: *(To Raya.)* You know, we have people like you in America. Homeless people—lots of them—in the subways. But they're nicer to us. You know? They don't lecture us. They're not angry like you. Some of them are crazy and drunk and on drugs, but they mind their own business. Maybe they're not as smart as you, but they know how to treat people. You could learn something from them.

RAYA: I'm not homeless. I have a home.

MAN: Yes. Why don't you go there. *(Patronizing her.)* Detochka.

JENNIFER: I think she called *me* that. What does it mean?

MAN: My dear little child.

JENNIFER: *(To Raya.)* Oh, you were being nice. I feel really bad now. It's just so hard to understand other people from other, you know, lands sometimes. *(Trying too hard to say it right.)* Dos Viy-dan-ya.

(Jennifer leaves with the Man.)

RAYA: *(To the audience.)* "And so I say unto you, the first shall become last and the last shall become first. And the merchants of the world shall weep over Babylon but all their fine goods will not save her. Behold, we come as thieves in the night and knock at your door. Blessed is he who is vigilant." *(Raya exits.)*

END OF PLAY

Breaking the Chain
by Michael Bigelow Dixon and
Val Smith

CHARACTERS

JESSICA: Mid-twenties, a skeptic.
CHUCK: Mid-twenties, a believer.
BETH: Mid-twenties, a believer.

TIME AND PLACE

Four days in the present.

Breaking the Chain

Lights up. Chuck is scraping wax off lottery tickets, and Beth is filling out coupons. Jessica watches from afar.

CHUCK: *(Sings.)* Luck be a lady tonight, luck be a lady tonight…

BETH: *(Sings.)* Dah da-da-da-da-da-da-da-da… da-da-da-da—

CHUCK AND BETH: *(A crescendo finish.)* Luck be a lady…*tonight!!!*

JESSICA: *(To audience.)* Chuck and Beth. My downstairs neighbors. Always doing nice things. Give me a ride when my car breaks down. I find a tuna casserole on my doorstep when I come home late from work. And when I'm sick, they show up at my bedside with Nyquil. So every once in awhile, I return the favor. *(To Chuck and Beth.)* Hey, guys, I got your mail.

BETH: Did you get it?

JESSICA: Get what?

CHUCK: *(Pulls out a letter.)* This.

JESSICA: What's this?

BETH: Open it. Oh, it's like Christmas.

JESSICA: *(Reads.)* "This letter has been around the world more than fifty times since it was first mailed in 1922." This is a joke, yes?

BETH: Give it to me! *(Reads enthusiastically.)* "One day when Sister Mary Margaret was tending the orchards at the Mission San Juan Capistrano, and feeding the swallows for which the Mission is famous…"

JESSICA: Great. We're going on vacation?

CHUCK: *(Joins in reading.)* "One such swallow came to light upon her hand."

BETH: "And Sister Mary Margaret noticed a little, tiny missive fastened to its little, tiny leg."

CHUCK: "It said, 'Eat Oranges.'"

JESSICA: Sounds like my mother.

CHUCK: "Following the note's advice, the good Sister sliced open an orange. And therein discovered the face of Baby Jesus."

JESSICA: I was right the first time. This *is* a joke.

BETH: "And then…Sister Mary Margaret heard the voice of Our Savior, commanding her to dig."

CHUCK: *(Commanding.)* Dig!

JESSICA: And up from the ground came a bubblin' crude!

BETH: "She discovered a cache of money, buried decades before."

JESSICA: I was close.

CHUCK: "And so the good Sister built her dream of a home for wayward girls."

BETH: "She began this letter so that others might share in her divine good fortune. Now you too can continue the Great Chain of Luck by mailing twenty copies of this letter within the next four days."

JESSICA: Not a chain letter.

BETH: Yes. And we sent it to you.

JESSICA: I mulch chain letters. Just my policy.

CHUCK: *(Stopping her.)* Ah-ah-ah. Lemme show you something. What do ya see?

JESSICA: A lottery ticket.

CHUCK: And?

JESSICA: Six oranges. *(Pause.)* So?

BETH: Oranges? Get it? Oranges!

JESSICA: *(Examining ticket.)* You won two dollars? Woo-wee!

CHUCK: The amount is irrelevant.

BETH: Though we do get a chance at the million dollar sweepstakes.

CHUCK: The point is we won. Right after we sent the letters off.

BETH: And now we've passed it along to you, continuing the Great Chain of Luck.

JESSICA: You're joking, of course.

CHUCK: Do you think we'd joke about Baby Jesus?

BETH: Sister Mary Margaret? And her bird?

CHUCK: Swallow.

JESSICA: I don't know how to break this to you. You bought what, look at that stack, what is it, fifty tickets? At a buck a pop. And you won two dollars. That's not luck, see. That's stupidity. Please. Don't do this to yourselves.

(Chuck and Beth share one of their laughs.)

JESSICA: What?

CHUCK: Tell her, Beth.

BETH: They called this morning. *(Hands Jessica a clipping.)*

JESSICA: The Bush Whackers Beauty Salon.

BETH: I won. There. See. I won!

JESSICA: A total beauty makeover. Do you really need one, Beth?

BETH: Well. I don't know. What do you think?

JESSICA: It's free. Might as well get your bush whacked.

CHUCK: The point is, out of all those people who filled out a coupon, all those who aspired to a total beauty makeover, it was Beth who won. More than random coincidence.

JESSICA: Divine intervention?

CHUCK AND BETH: Yes!

JESSICA: *(To audience.)* Sad. I wanted to slap them. But I thought "Give 'em a day. They'll come to their senses."

CHUCK: Good morning.

BETH: How are you?

CHUCK: We're worried about you.

BETH: Have you sent the letters?

JESSICA: Are we still on this—this—what's this?

(Beth hands Jessica another lottery ticket.)

CHUCK: A thousand dollars.

BETH: And another chance at the million!

JESSICA: Congratulations. All right. Look. I'm happy for you. Satisfied? Now, can't we, as friends, just agree to disagree about this?

BETH: Jessica—

JESSICA: No. There's no point in trotting out any more of those rotten little tote bags, or wrench sets, or whatever else you've won—

CHUCK: A Chris Craft Cabin Cruiser.

JESSICA: Whatever—to make me jealous. It's a matter of principle. I mean, if everybody started believing in this stuff, before you know it, we'd be back in the Middle Ages. Hiding from eclipses.

BETH: Jessica.

JESSICA: Torching people at the stake!

CHUCK: Jessica!

JESSICA: I'm sorry. I'm a skeptic. So sue me. By the way, the Cabin Cruiser should look terrific in your driveway.

BETH: Actually we're keeping it in the boathouse.

JESSICA: Boathouse.

CHUCK: Part of the dream estate on Lake Tahoe.

JESSICA: I don't want to know.

BETH: Don't be upset, Jess. We'll be here for most of the year.

JESSICA: Okay. So the law of averages has been pulling in your favor a little more lately. That is all.

CHUCK: Send your copies out.

JESSICA: I'm too busy. I do not have the time.

BETH: We'll do it for you. Here are the envelopes.

JESSICA: I'm out of stamps!

CHUCK: WE got 'em! We can afford 'em.

JESSICA: I don't know twenty people!

BETH: *(Slapping down a phone book.)* You don't have to! Send 'em to people you don't know.

CHUCK: Send 'em to people you don't like!

BETH: But send 'em!

CHUCK AND BETH: PULLLLEEEEEZZZZE!

JESSICA: Why is this so important to you?

BETH: Because we love you, Jessica.

JESSICA: Well, gee, I love you guys, too.

CHUCK: And we fear for your life.

JESSICA: *(To audience.)* Then they read me the rest of the letter.

BETH: *(Reads.)* "Be warned."

CHUCK: *(Reads.)* "Those who have broken the chain have suffered dire consequences. Melissa Cantrow did not pass on twenty copies of this letter within four days. At a church retreat, she was struck in the head with an arrow by a mentally challenged inner-city auto mechanic."

JESSICA: Ouch.

BETH: "Elizabeth Swanson failed to pass on this letter. She contracted herpes. A week later, a basset hound bit off her nose."

JESSICA: There's a candidate for the Bush Whackers.

BETH: It's serious.

CHUCK: "Within a month after not responding, Alfred Nosinger was divorced from his wife. And his left buttock was sliced off in an amusement park accident."

JESSICA: Okay. I get the picture.

BETH: And Sister Mary Margaret signed it, "*Alea iacta est.*"

CHUCK: The die is cast, Jessica. The clock is ticking.

BETH: *Tempus fugit.*

JESSICA: *(To audience.)* Time flies. And so did I. Fugit. Right out of there. Beth and Chuck are good people, I thought. Solid citizens, middle Americans, and my friends. Yet, clearly, they'd gone insane. It can't last, I thought. In the meantime, avoid them. Out of sight. Out of mind.

(Jessica exits. Chuck and Beth sit at their table and open mail.)

CHUCK: *(Depressed.)* Today's mail. *(Opens a letter, reads without pleasure.)* We won the trip to Cancun.

BETH: *(Also depressed.)* The raffle for the tornado victims. We won the new mobile home.

CHUCK: Set of ginzu knives.

BETH: An authentic zirconian diamond in a simulated gold setting.

CHUCK: *(Still without enthusiasm.)* Looks real.

BETH: Chuck?

CHUCK: I know. I know.

(Phone rings.)

BETH: What good is all of this if Jessica loses a buttock?

CHUCK: *(On phone.)* Hello? Yes it is. Thank you, we will. *(Hangs up.)*

CHUCK AND BETH: *(Together.)* The Ford Bronco. *(They sigh.)*

BETH: We can't just keep sitting here and winning things.

CHUCK: I know. This must be what hell is like. *(Opens envelope.)*

BETH: Free tree pruning.

CHUCK: A year's supply of Little Debbie Snack Cakes.

BETH: She's avoiding us. We've got to get to her. Somehow. Some way. What's that?

CHUCK: A free Mr. Potato Head. Damn! I'm so upset I can't even enjoy this! *(Throws Mr. Potato Head.)*

BETH: Wait. Footsteps.

(Beth throws open the door revealing Jessica tiptoeing past.)

JESSICA: Hi, how ya doin'?

(Beth and Chuck stare at Jessica.)

JESSICA: What? Why are you staring? Is there something on my pants?

BETH: God I'm gonna miss that buttock.

JESSICA: Stop it! Stop that!

BETH: *(Beginning to cry.)* I'm sorry.

JESSICA: Chuck? Are you aware that things have gotten a bit out of hand here?

CHUCK: I have two words to say. Bassett. Hound.

JESSICA: Can we please change the subject? What happened to the days we used to sit around and shoot the breeze? Chew the tuna casserole?

BETH: *(Crying.)* We're going to miss you so much.

JESSICA: Help me, Chuck.

CHUCK: That's what we've been trying to do, Jessica. If you could just think of it as simple economics. Your car payments, your rent…

BETH: You need a new wardrobe.

JESSICA: Gee. Thanks.

CHUCK: What I'm saying is, Jessica, stop acting like a tard.

JESSICA: I'm not sending them out! End of topic.

> *(Doorbell rings.)*

BETH: I'll get it. *(Beth exits.)*

JESSICA: So, can we talk about work? We used to talk about work. In the good old days. Work. Right. So, how's work, Chuck?

CHUCK: I plan to retire.

JESSICA: Oh really?

> *(Beth reenters.)*

CHUCK: What is it, Beth?

JESSICA: What's the matter?

BETH: *(Pause.)* WE WON! WE WON! WE WON A MILLION DOLLARS!!!!

CHUCK: YEAHHHHHHH! I quit! I quit! I quit!

> *(The sound of clock chimes.)*

CHUCK AND BETH: Oh my God! The fifth day!

BETH: Chuck, she looks feverish.

CHUCK: You don't think—?

BETH: Herpes?

JESSICA: That's it. I'm leaving.

BETH: Don't go!

JESSICA: I'm moving out!

CHUCK: Stop! What would it take to make you believe?

JESSICA: A miracle.

BETH: Well, just look at everything we won.

JESSICA: A real miracle. That orange. Cut it in half.

CHUCK: No fair!

JESSICA: Look, I don't know how to explain what's happening here, but I know I don't want anything to do with it. You guys are out of the box.

CHUCK: Out of the box!!!

BETH: What box?

CHUCK: Give me that orange.

BETH: No, Chuck. She won't believe. She'll never believe. Jessica is lost!

CHUCK: *(Cutting the orange in half and holding it up.)* There! See!!!!

BETH: The Baby Jesus!

JESSICA: Where? Where? Where is Baby Jesus?

CHUCK: *(Pointing first to one half, then the other.)* Right there. Right there. Both halves! Stereo!!!!

JESSICA: Certifiable psychos.

BETH: Yeah? Well, I hope you lose both buttocks.

CHUCK: I hope you lose your whole ass!

(Chuck and Beth exit. Jessica is left alone on stage.)

JESSICA: What happens to people?…And when they're your friends? …My friends…I mean, hey, somebody had to win. Pure mathematics. Not luck, definitely not brains. *(Pause.)* But that letter. Sister Mary Margaret, the terrorist nun. I'm sorry, I don't buy it. If somebody wins, why does somebody have to lose? Hogwash. I did the right thing. 'Cause if there's one principle by which I live, that's standing up—no, sitting down—for what I don't believe in.

(Jessica crumples chain letter and tosses it aside. An arrow lands on stage and a bassett hound bays—perhaps her chair collapses. Blackout.)

END OF PLAY

Night Visits
by Simon Fill

CHARACTERS

TOM: A second-year resident in medicine, twenty-eight.

LIZ: A nurse, twenty-seven.

EMILY: Gentle, looks about twenty-three.

TIME

The present.

LOCATION

An examination room in a hospital.

Night Visits

A hospital examination room. White. Patient gowns hang all over. We hear wind outside. Tom lies on the examining table, asleep. Twenty-eight. In a doctor's outfit. Liz enters. Twenty-seven. Nurse's uniform. Quiet moment to herself, then notices the gowns and Tom.

TOM: *(Eyes closed.)* I'm not seeing patients anymore, Liz. *(Quickly, lightly, sounding upbeat and energetic.)* It's over. It's over. It's over. It's over. It's over. It's over. It's over. It's over. It's over. It's over. It's over. It's over. It's over. It's over. It's over. It's over. Do you have a problem with it being over? You better not. Is it not really over? I don't think so.

LIZ: Tom. One more. That's all.

TOM: Seeing one patient in your thirty-fifth hour of being awake is the equivalent of seeing fifteen hundred in your first.

LIZ: You can't refuse to see patients. You're a resident.

TOM: Shit.

(He gets up.)

TOM: You look…nice.

LIZ: Got a date.

TOM: Doctor?

LIZ: No.

TOM: Yes. Yes. YES! Good for *you*.

LIZ: You are such a freak. *(Looks out window.)* Windy outside.

TOM: It's a bad night.

LIZ: I know. We all do.

TOM: …What? Oh. I'm…fine.

LIZ: We all loved Katie, Tom.

TOM: Yeah. Thanks. No, I mean it.

LIZ: She was a great nurse. I wish I'd known her more.

TOM: You're okay, Liz. I hate to admit it.

(He hits her lightly on the arm.)

LIZ: You are such a freak. *(Beat.)* This patient—Doug gave her a shot of methicillin, he's busy now. Watch her ten minutes, see if she's allergic. She was… in a car…

TOM: Look. Katie's accident was a year ago.

LIZ: To the day.

TOM: I'm not really doing anything to this patient anyhow.

LIZ: You mean that?

TOM: *(Very dramatic.)* Have I *ever* lied to you before?

LIZ: Yeah.

TOM: No, 'bout something serious.

LIZ: Yeah.

TOM: You're—you're—you're—
(Jokingly, he grabs a tiny knee hammer.)

LIZ: You gonna test my reflexes? You are such a…!

TOM: What!

LIZ: *(Beat. Softly, with great fondness.)* Little boy. This patient. The accident involved only her. After it, she disappeared. They found her in a church. Sitting on the floor. Surrounded herself with lit wish candles. Hundreds. She'd been there hours. When they asked her why, she said, "I'm cold."
(She gives him a chart. He stares at her.)

LIZ: Emily. I know, I know. She's odd, this one. Another sweet nobody. Passed a psych consult, but otherwise, she won't talk. Here twenty-one hours. Won't leave till she feels she's "okay." She's a little banged up, but fine. She could go now. She won't. Bring her upstairs when you're done. *(Beat. Studies Tom with suspicion.)* No.

TOM: I'm good at this. She'll feel better. She'll leave.

LIZ: Won't work. We tried everything. Social services was called. They'll be here soon. *(Looks at robes.)* I wish we had another free room.

TOM: You didn't carry those up from a broken dryer at three in the morning.

LIZ: Dr. Pitnick, that was nice. Someday you'll make a good nurse.

TOM: I'll get her to go.

LIZ: Won't happen. *(Looks him up and down.)* You need a compliment. Badly. *(Beat.)* Serious now. You okay?

TOM: Funny. When Katie died, I prayed every night for a month.

LIZ: What about?

TOM: If I told anyone, Liz, I'd tell you. *(Lightly.)* It was very self-involved. *(Beat.)* I'm fine. Thanks. Have a good date. You're not as cute as you think you are.

LIZ: *(Smiles.)* I'll send her down. See you tomorrow.

(She exits. Pause. The sound of wind. He looks out the window. He is overcome and starting to break down. A knock. He recovers himself.)

TOM: *(Cheerful.)* Dr. Pitnick's house of optimism and laundry!

(Emily enters. She looks about twenty-three. Gentle. Bruised face and arms.)

TOM: *(Grins. A quick patter. His routine.)* Just kidding. There's no optimism here. Don't mean to be unprofessional. I expect you to stay silent. *(Looks at chart, then her arm, checking where the shot was given.)* Hope that didn't hurt too much. I hate shots. We're gonna get you to feel okay. I usually do this by showing patients how impressive they are in comparison to me. Some patients protest. For good reason. I expect you to stay silent. They call me the funny doctor. *(To self.)* This is like one of my dates in high school. *(Looks at her.)* Did I detect a glint of humanity?

(She smiles a little.)

TOM: I bet no one upstairs tried to crack you up. Their mistake. Do you feel sorry for yourself?

(She shakes her head.)

TOM: You ought to. You gotta listen to me. But if you talk to me, you get to listen to me less. 'Round here, I'm considered aversion therapy for introverts. *(Whispers.)* Of course, being the funniest doctor 'round here is a weak claim. *(Beat. Back to normal.)* Look. I know what you went through was serious. I know. I do. But sometimes when you think you're alone, when you most think that, you…aren't. *(Beat.)* Sorry. I'm expecting a lot here. I mean, it's not like you're God or anything. No offense.

(Silence. He raises his hands in surrender, looks out the window. Pause.)

EMILY: Why would I be offended you don't think I'm God? That's pretty queer.

TOM: I'm not the one who surrounded myself with wish candles in a church.

EMILY: Does that unnerve you? Dr. Tom?

TOM: *(Beat.)* How'd you know my name was Tom?

EMILY: *(Mock mystical.)* Woo woo.

(Beat. She points at his name tag.)

TOM: Oh. Wow. I need some sleep. Sorry. I shouldn't say that.

EMILY: *(Lightly teasing.)* C'mon. This is all about you. *(Beat. Sincere.)* You look tired. You okay?

TOM: Great. My patient's asking me if I'm okay. Are you?

EMILY: You want me to leave, don't you?

TOM: I… *(Looks at her face and arms. Gentle.)* These bruises'll disappear on their own in a few days. They hurt?

EMILY: No, they feel great. Sorry. Not that bad. Thanks. You're nice.

TOM: I'm only nice when I'm tired.

EMILY: How often you tired?

TOM: Always. You're gonna be fine.

EMILY: I'm not important. What?

TOM: Nothing.

EMILY: What?

TOM: *(Warmly ironic.)* I WISH someone'd said that in your chart!
    (She smiles.)

EMILY: You're weird.

TOM: I know.

EMILY: When the accident happened, I hit a divider, everything stopped. I didn't
    know where I was. For some reason, I thoughta my dad. He died four
    years ago. Nothing to do with cars. I…loved him. After he was gone, I
    never felt his loss. I… Something happened.
    (Pause.)

TOM: You tell anyone this?

EMILY: Do you count? *(Beat.)* I got out of the car, looked around to make sure
    no one was hurt. Then I ran.
    (Silence.)
    You all right?

TOM: Yeah. Sure. I'm gonna get you outta here. In good shape.

EMILY: *(Lightly.)* I'm a nobody. And I dress poorly.

TOM: What's the one thing you could do to give your life meaning?

EMILY: Accessorize?
    (Beat. He smiles. She looks off.)

EMILY: You can't see wind.

TOM: What?

EMILY: You can't see it, but it's there.

TOM: *(Beat.)* Is it? When the accident happened, who were you with?

EMILY: That's an odd question.

TOM: Who were you with?

EMILY: Why?

TOM: Answer it!

EMILY: No one! *(Beat.)* I was hurt, and for the first time I felt, *knew*, I'm with
    no one. My father, he's really… gone…
    (Pause.)
    You understand what I'm saying?

TOM: *(Thinks with care, then nods slowly.)* I'm sorry. *(Beat.)* You okay?

EMILY: *(Upset. Snippy.)* With doctors like you, who needs accidents!

TOM: Sorry.

EMILY: I… No, don't feel bad for me. I don't. My father… I loved him.

TOM: Did he love you?

EMILY: Yes, but that's not as important.

TOM: You okay?

EMILY: Keep asking that, and you won't be.

TOM: *(Softly.)* Sorry.

EMILY: Stop apologizing, you didn't kill him. *(Beat.)* When I left the accident, a few blocks away I passed a homeless woman. I asked her for the nearest good church. One that was honest, that wasn't about exclusion. She said nothing. I asked again, and she goes, "Here."
(She points to her heart.)

TOM: *(Softly.)* Oh.

EMILY: You enjoy helping this nobody?

TOM: Who? You?

EMILY: You know a lot about this. *(Beat.)* Who was it?

TOM: You're my patient.

EMILY: So? There's doctor-patient privilege. I won't tell anyone.

TOM: I'm trying to make *you* all right.

EMILY: You're almost there. This'll help. Or don't you open up to nobodies?

TOM: Is this a trick?

EMILY: Yes. You got me to like you.

TOM: *(Beat.)* My wife, Katherine. She was a nurse here in pediatrics. We grew up together in Brooklyn, but in high school I was too shy to ask her out. We ran into each other when she'd graduated from college, at a reading of James Joyce by an Irish actor. Joyce was her favorite writer. She and I dated. At that point, I was well on my way to becoming the "funny doctor." She was quiet and funnier, in that good way the most serious people are. After two months, I proposed. Now that was funny. She didn't answer. We kept dating. Every day for two months after that I proposed. Silence. I thought, "This woman either likes me or is totally insensate." At the end of that time she gave me a copy of *Finnegan's Wake*, her favorite book. At college I'd read it and almost finished. The first page, that is. But I loved her so much I slogged through the book. Boy, did I love her. On page fifty, at the bottom, in pencil, someone'd written something. I looked closely. It said, "Yes. I'll marry you."
(Pause.)

I called her up and told her Joyce had accepted my proposal of marriage. *(Pause.)*

She was driving to Riverdale, a favor, to pick up a friend's kid at school. I know she was starting to think about children herself. She said she wanted them to have "my looks and her sense of humor." Another car, an old lady who shouldn't have been driving, who had a history of epilepsy…and…you know the rest. The other woman lived. *(Beat.)* I asked Katie once why she wrote yes to me on page fifty. She said, "I knew you loved me, but I wasn't sure how much." *(Pause.)* Don't look so serious.

EMILY: *(Gently.)* The line you draw between yourself and other people, it doesn't exist. Not how you think. You know that, you'll let her inside of you, even if she's gone.

TOM: *(Softly.)* Hey. Thanks.

EMILY: *(With affection.)* You gonna believe that? Or are you just another punk doctor?

(Long pause.)

TOM: Yeah, I do. *(Beat.)* Yeah. *(Beat.)* What do you charge? I don't know if my insurance covers this.

EMILY: This was good.

TOM: I can't treat you for premature nostalgia. It isn't my specialty. You gonna stay or go?

EMILY: Quiet in here.

TOM: *(Light. Gentle.)* That tough being a nobody?

(She smiles.)

TOM: Funny. When Katie died, I prayed every night for a month. It was very self-involved.

EMILY: No, it was just about her. You asked that she be okay. You never worried about yourself. That's incredibly rare, even for people who love each other. *And* you're a nonbeliever.

TOM: *(Beat.)* How'd you know that?

EMILY: Who listens to prayers?

TOM: I don't get it.

EMILY: Who listens to prayers?

TOM: Nobody! *(Beat. A slow realization.)* Nobody. You could leave the hospital now.

EMILY: Thanks for the permission.

(She gathers her things.)

EMILY: Oh, and Tom?

TOM: Yeah?

EMILY: Your insurance doesn't cover it.

(She leaves. Pause. The sound of wind. He looks out the window. He opens it. When the wind enters the room, the robes fill with air, as if inhabited by ghosts. They sway beautifully. Tableau. Blackout.)

END OF PLAY

One Hundred Women
by Kristina Halvorson

CHARACTERS

NINA

KELLY

CHRISTIAN

TIME AND PLACE

The present.
Nina and Kelly's apartment.

One Hundred Women

Lights up on Nina who is standing center stage. As the poem is spoken (voice-over—it is Nina's voice), she begins a graceful dance comprised mostly of gesture and facial expression. Her movements are reaction to the words, not a pantomime.

NINA: "My hazard wouldn't be yours, not ever;
But every doom, like a hazelnut, comes down
To its own worm. So I am rocking here
Like any granny with her apron over her head
Saying, lordy me. It's my trouble.
There's nothing to be learned this way.
If I heard a girl crying help
I would go to save her;
But you hardly ever hear those words.
Dear children, you must try to say
Something when you are in need.
Don't confuse hunger with greed;
And don't wait until you are dead."[1]

(Lights down. Lights up on Nina at a small kitchen table. She is surrounded by books, notecards, highlighters, notebooks, etc. She is obviously buried in work. Kelly runs in. She is distracted and in a hurry.)

NINA: *(Without looking up.)* Say, didn't you used to live around here? Like, with me?

KELLY: *(Kissing her head or cheek as she passes.)* Hi, friend—I can't stay, gotta get to the coffee shop before Christian gives up on me for good and leaves…

NINA: Did you make it to class today?

---

[1] "Advice" written by Ruth Stone. Used by permission of the author.

KELLY: No—damn, where are my keys?—Christian and I were up so late last night—you know the hours he keeps since he quit school—I keep meaning to spend the night here sometime this week so I can have at least one productive morning—

NINA: How's everything going? Are you doing okay?

KELLY: *(Distracted, running around.)* Sure, say, have you washed out that sweater of mine you borrowed?

NINA: No, I haven't gotten around to it. Listen, why don't we...

KELLY: God, I've got to go—Nina, would you mind...

NINA: *(Interrupting her.)* Well, no, nothing's new really. Oh, I meant to tell you—the pregnancy test came up positive, but I've narrowed down the possible fathers to six contenders—

KELLY: What?

NINA: Other than that I haven't been too busy—I've given up the whole master's program, changed religions, changed my name, bought a house in the country...

KELLY: Nina...

NINA: Wait, I've forgotten something... learned to tap, knit a sweater, voted Republican, ate tomatoes on my sandwich at lunch for the first time in my life, and inherited a ranch in South Dakota. Other than that my schedule's been pretty open. How've you been? Fine, thanks for asking. Good of you to stop by. We'll see you next month. Knock yourself out. *(Turns back to her work.)*

KELLY: *(Pause.)* Nina? *(Pause.)* Are you mad at me?

NINA: God, Kelly...

KELLY: *(Snaps back into action.)* Look, we'll talk, but later, I've got to go. *(Another kiss.)* I miss you. You're insane. Wait up for me tonight, huh? I'll try to make it home. *(Exits.)*

NINA: Yeah. Whatever. Say hi to Christian. Bastard.
  (Lights change. Nina addresses the audience.)

NINA: I've lived with Kelly for two years now; this is our third. We do well together because our lives are so different—we don't ask much of each other, nor do we expect much—so when we're able to give each other attention, any attention, it's welcomed, if not necessarily needed. For the most part I consider myself a strong woman. I'd like to think I don't need much from anyone. People find that admirable. You know, I think it's actually gotten to the point where even if I did discover I needed anything from her, I wouldn't know how to ask. We're grownups, for God's sakes.

Companionship should be an extra, not a focus. I have a career to build. She's just my roommate.

We've lived in this quiet realm of no demands for so long, this place of easy peace. There have been months, hundreds of days when I asked nothing from her. But now something has changed. Suddenly I'm lonely. Suddenly I want her near me. Suddenly, in place of our peace, there's a silence waiting to be filled. I wonder if she can hear it.

I don't think she's stopped lately to listen.

(Lights change. Christian is on the floor, staring at the ceiling. Kelly is sitting and watching him, ignoring the book in her hand. Nina stands up from her work, steps over Christian.)

NINA: Can I get you anything, Christian? Coffee? Tea? A job?

KELLY: Nina.

CHRISTIAN: *(Without moving or changing focus.)* Nina, Nina, queen of my heart.

NINA: *(Beat as she stares at Christian.)* Excuse me. *(Goes to the edge of the stage, stands, and watches the scene evolve. May react physically, might sit down later. Although visible to the audience, she is out of the scene, and Kelly and Christian are alone.)*

KELLY: Christian. Christian. *(Moves to him, touches him, flirts a little.)* What is it? It's me, isn't it. *(Deadpan.)* You want me. You want me desperately to…

CHRISTIAN: *(Without moving.)* I want you to move in with me.

KELLY: Christian…

CHRISTIAN: Why do you stay here, Kelly? Your rent is outrageous, you stay over at my place six days out of the week anyhow, and your roommate's a bitch.

KELLY: *(Her usual speech.)* Christian, she's just been under a lot of pressure…

CHRISTIAN: So it's my fault she's having a nervous breakdown? *I* can't even deal with her anymore, and *you're* the one living with her. She's an over-achieving, self-righteous, sexually repressed feminazi. Why is she always on me? 'Cause I'm a *guy?* It's like she blames me for having a life.

KELLY: I'm not sure she sees it quite like that.

CHRISTIAN: Well, my God, when was the last time she went out with anyone? Even you? When was the last time she put down her precious books and took a good look at you, asked you how you're doing, what's in your heart? *(Pause.)* Kelly. Look. I want you to come home with me. I want my bed to be our bed. I want to shop for groceries with you, do laundry with you, argue about who's going to clean the crap out of the sink drain. I want you beside me every morning when I open my eyes. I want your legs wrapped around my waist at night when I fall asleep. Don't you want that? Why wouldn't you want that?

KELLY: *(Pause. Quietly.)* I don't want to move out of my home, Christian. Nina and I do well together. There's an understanding—if I need her—we both—God, why do you keep asking me this? Don't ask me this. Nina is my family here.

CHRISTIAN: You never see her.

KELLY: That's not the point. If I needed to, I would. She'd be there.

CHRISTIAN: Kel, I'm here.

KELLY: Christian, that's different—

CHRISTIAN: Why? Can you tell me why?

KELLY: Christian. *(Pause.)* Look, I'll think about it.

CHRISTIAN: *(Simply.)* I love you.

KELLY: I'll think about it.

CHRISTIAN: *(Resigned.)* What the hell.

(Pause. The discussion is over. He kisses her. She responds. They rise up to their knees. He kisses her neck, then places his ear to her chest. She holds him. He listens.)

CHRISTIAN: That's so weird. *(He takes his hand and places it in three or four places on her left breast, searching for her heartbeat.)* I give up. I can never find a woman's heartbeat.

(Kelly gently places his hand where her heartbeat should be. He waits, then shakes his head. Lights fade on Christian and Kelly, remain up on Nina.)

NINA: I think about them a lot. I think about the time they spend together; about what movies they watch, where they might go for dinner, if he's good in bed—but I especially think about the time they spend lying around, watching TV, doing nothing together, when I so desperately want to be doing something, together, with her. Anything. God.

I've started to wonder if I'm in love with her. But as I say it out loud I realize how ridiculous it sounds, how impossible it would be. "Kelly, I know I've been a little clingy lately, and well, frankly, I want to go to bed with you." That's not what I want. I don't know what I want. What I know is that I'm empty, and lonely, and that she fills me up like no one else can, male or female. The way we can talk, how hard we can laugh, how easily we make up each other's home. Used to.

I think I'm getting desperate. For some reason the only way I can imagine getting her to spend more time with me is to seduce her. But in the end, what would I say to her once the lights came back on?

(Lights change. Kelly enters, distracted and hurried. Nina explodes.)

NINA: Where the hell have you been? You were due back this morning—I thought we were going for breakfast—I called Christian's about eight times and no one answered—I missed the first twenty minutes of my two o'clock seminar because I was calling all the hospitals and police stations looking for you!

KELLY: Jesus, Nina, I'm sorry, Christian and I were just up last night hashing some stuff out so—

NINA: Could you have called?

KELLY: I was sleeping.

NINA: Sleeping? You were sleep…it was noon on a Tuesday and you were asleep? What are you doing, Kel? Why are you doing this to yourself? You are in school. You have certain responsibilities you've accepted…

KELLY: Look, the last thing I need is—

NINA: I *know* what you need—

KELLY: How can you say that? How can you even *begin* to—

NINA: Kelly, don't do this, I'm only—

KELLY: All I'm saying is—

NINA: All I'm saying is that I'd appreciate it if…

KELLY: Nina!

NINA: …*if* in the future you'd show me some consideration.

KELLY: You know, where's the part when you stop acting like my goddamn mother? I don't even recognize you right now.

NINA: I don't understand what is so awful about my simply wanting to know—

KELLY: Nina, *stop it.* Can you stop it? Are you capable? My God, please, just… stop.

NINA: *(Pause.)* I didn't know where you were. It was so bright outside. Everyone had their windows down, their car stereos blaring—there were a hundred people on their way to class or to work, talking and smiling— and I was standing at the kitchen sink, staring out the window in the middle of broad daylight, wondering if you were dead.

KELLY: This is ridiculous. *(Pause.)* Nina. I'm sorry. I'm sorry I didn't call. I'm okay. I can take care of myself. I'm not going to do anything stupid. I'm sorry.

NINA: I just didn't know what to do with this, this panic. It was in me, all through me, Kelly, and I—

KELLY: It's okay. *(Pause. They do not move toward each other.)* It's all right.
(Lights change. Kelly turns away from Nina, walks toward the edge of the stage, where Christian comes to meet her. They slowly go to their knees and resume their previous position, Christian's hand on Kelly's chest, his head tilted as he waits to feel her heartbeat. The light on them is dim. Focus on Nina, who has not moved since Kelly's last line. She speaks as soon as Kelly reaches Christian.)

NINA: There is a place, inside me, where one hundred women live. It is full of light and anything but lonely. I keep Kelly there, and my mother, and my third-grade teacher, Mrs. Rhodes, and my best friend, Christine, from eighth grade, and all the other women who have touched me somehow. There are so many. I close my eyes and I imagine them sitting close together in interlocked circles, talking, holding each other, laughing. Inside me, they know one another. Perhaps some of them are the same. When I am alone I laugh along with them, wrap my arms tight around my breasts, hugging myself, drawing them closer to me. It's only when the men invite themselves in—into the room, into the laughter, even into me—that the links of this, this woman chain are weakened. The men call, and the women come. The circles break apart. I begin to feel like I am coming apart, that my parts are loose and dangling. I hug myself even tighter and rename, reimagine my women. There is at least one hundred of me, without them, I think—Nina the scholar, Nina the poet, the student, the counselor, the lover. I wait for the strongest one of me to step forward so that I can find the right words, summon up the elusive courage to bring back the women I've somehow lost.

And yet, despite my frantic attempts to call forth the philosopher, the diplomat, the encouraging friend, somehow it is always Nina the lover who wins out. She gives in to the romance, releases the women to their princes and saviors. Her mother remarries, her schoolteacher moves away with her husband, her best friend falls head over heels for a ninth grader. And Nina the lover nods; Nina the lover knows. She lowers her head and waits for her turn to come, and in the meantime the women fall away from her one by one by one by one…

What can I do but embrace her, this lover who lives inside my chest, and bid farewell to the other ninety-nine of me, who always retreat in silence.

How difficult can it be to call out the name of a friend you're terrified of losing?

(Lights up on Christian and Kelly. He still has his hand on Kelly's heart. Nina walks over to them and places her hand next to Christian's. Neither Christian nor Kelly move.)

NINA: *(To Christian.)* I can feel it. *(To Kelly.)* Do you hear me, Kelly? I found it. I can feel it.

END OF PLAY

Lonely
by Ann Marie Healy

CHARACTERS
FRANK: Late twenties.

MILLY: Late twenties.

FRANCES: Milly's sister, early twenties.

PLACE
Frank and Milly's living room.

Lonely

Frank, Milly, and Frances enter the living room.

MILLY: And this is the living room. This is where we do the living.

FRANK: The living. Right. A man needs to live. In a room.

FRANCES: It's great.

MILLY: It is great.

FRANK: This is a great place to sit and think. Sometimes I come in here and think to myself.

MILLY: Or you think out loud.

FRANK: True. I might think out loud. If Milly's in here, I think out loud and she listens. *(To himself.)* I think that I used to be scared of the winter. *(To Milly and Frances.)* You see, I'm thinking out loud right now.

MILLY: *(To Frances.)* It's so dark—the winter, that's what he means. *(To Frank.)* Is that what you mean?

FRANK: Sort of. More cold than dark. You were close.

FRANCES: At least it's warm inside your house.

MILLY: Right. Frank sits there and I sit here and we get a big stack of wood from outside and make a fire.

FRANK: Cozy. It's very cozy. That's living.

MILLY: I make Hot Toddies sometimes. We never let it get cold like Mom and Dad's. Mom would never serve a Hot Toddy.

FRANK: Homebodies. That's how I've always liked to fancy myself. *(Frank grabs Milly and kisses her.)* I'll tell you though, it's a lot more fun being a homebody when there's another body there.

MILLY: I'm the body! I'm the body!

FRANK: She's the body. I'm the brains.

FRANCES: Right, right!

FRANK: That was my joke.

MILLY: No. He's the brawn. He's the muscle that turns the corks. Or the screws. Or…how does that saying go?

FRANCES: What saying?

MILLY: The saying about making the machinery go?

FRANK: Oh…right. Right. She means I make the machinery go. *(Pause.)* Are you talking about my tool shop?

MILLY: Well…yes. But also in a larger sense.

FRANCES: Milly is always thinking in a larger sense.

MILLY: Why do you say that?

FRANCES: Your mind never rests on the situation at hand.

MILLY: That's not true.

FRANK: What is the larger sense of my tool shop?

MILLY: There is no larger sense, Frank.

FRANK: Right, right. Have you been downstairs, Frances?

FRANCES: Not yet.

MILLY: The other day Frank spent the entire morning—well you tell it. I can't tell it.

FRANK: The other day I what?

MILLY: You spent the day in the basement and…You tell the story. I can't tell stories.

FRANK: Oh…we don't need to tell that story.

MILLY: But it's funny.

FRANK: *(Holds up hand to reveal a bandage around his finger.)* The ending is no fun. It wasn't really that funny.

MILLY: *(Pause.)* Right. The ending is no fun. *(To Frances.)* It was funny at the time though.

FRANCES: I'm sure. I can sort of imagine it.

MILLY: You can?

FRANCES: I mean the part about the basement.

MILLY: Good.

FRANCES: I can imagine it being very funny.

(Pause.)

MILLY: Frank, put on some music will you?

FRANK: Something fast? Something slow?

MILLY: Frank likes bongos.

FRANK: Likes? Loves.

FRANCES: Something slow.

(Frank exits. Music plays softly. Milly and Frances stand in silence.)

MILLY: You're not happy.

FRANCES: Sure I am.

MILLY: What's wrong?

FRANCES: Nothing's wrong.

MILLY: Are you lonely?

FRANCES: No.

MILLY: I thought you might be lonely.

FRANCES: Not very.

MILLY: Well if you are...don't be.

FRANCES: All right.

MILLY: Now you're being sarcastic.

FRANCES: I'm not.

MILLY: You know what it is don't you?

FRANCES: What what is?

MILLY: The reason.

FRANCES: No.

MILLY: *(Whispering.)* Mom and Dad are getting older.

FRANCES: So are you.

MILLY: Well so are you. You'll have to leave home sometime.

FRANCES: I like it there.

MILLY: That's what I thought too. Then I left. And now *(She motions around the room.)* I have this. *(Pause.)* Do you know Frank and I put a couch in our bedroom? I've always wanted to put a couch in my bedroom, and he said to just do it and now when I walk into the bedroom he says "Hey you! Come sit on the bed." And then I walk over and sit on the couch. You know why? Because they're both in my bedroom.

FRANCES: I have my bedroom the way I like it. There's not much clutter. *(Pause.)* People are clutter.

MILLY: Only the wrong person is clutter. The right person is the treat at the end of the long maze. The reward for being lost! Maybe you're lost, Frances. *(Pause.)*

FRANCES: I have been talking to myself lately.

MILLY: You always talk to yourself.

FRANCES: But lately, I've been...responding to myself in a different voice.

MILLY: What kind of voice?

FRANCES: *(Pause.)* There are a few...different voices. Some are...rowdier than others.

MILLY: Frances.

FRANCES: What?

MILLY: You're lonely.

FRANCES: So?

MILLY: What ever happened to Bill?

FRANCES: Bob?

MILLY: Bob.

FRANCES: Nothing.

MILLY: Why?

FRANCES: *(Pause.)* I made him up.

MILLY: What?

FRANCES: And Chuck and Mo and Phillip…

MILLY: All of them?

FRANCES: Yes.

MILLY: But they weren't even nice to you. Didn't Mo cheat on you?

FRANCES: Twice… Once with Phillip.

MILLY: Why did you lie?

FRANCES: So I would have something to talk about…with you.

MILLY: We have things to talk about Frances…. Don't we?

FRANCES: I don't know.

> *(Pause.)*

MILLY: What did you do all those nights?

FRANCES: I went to the movies. I went to diners. I walked around. I did things. That's what I'm trying to tell you, Milly. I have a lot of fun.

MILLY: What kind of fun?

FRANCES: I just told you.

MILLY: Oh. *(Pause.)* Well it's not the worst thing.

FRANCES: What?

MILLY: Being lonely.

FRANCES: I know.

MILLY: No you don't. It's not the worst thing because it makes everything better in the end.

FRANCES: What end?

MILLY: The end of the maze. That thing that you find when you're lonely.

FRANCES: Thing?

MILLY: Frank.

FRANCES: *(Pause.)* Oh.

> *(Frank returns from the other room.)*

FRANK: There's a particular bongo that plays in the background of this song. Shhh… Everybody listen.

> *(They stop for a moment to listen.)*

FRANCES: I don't hear it.

FRANK: Neither do I. That's funny…I'm sure it's there.

MILLY: Your hearing is going. In your old age.

FRANK: My old age... I was calculating my years last night, and I spent the majority of my life unhappy. *(Frank turns to Frances.)* Do you know I spent the majority of my life unhappy?

MILLY: Frances is unhappy right now.

FRANK: Are you?

FRANCES: I never said that.

MILLY: She's lonely.

FRANK: Frances.... Are you lonely? I was lonely too. Really. *(Pause.)* I would say seven-eighths of my life I was lonely because for that amount of time, divided up mathematically, I was without your sister.

FRANCES: I know. You did the math in your marriage proposal.

FRANK: My proposal. Frances, how do you think I fancied myself that day?

FRANCES: I remember your suit.

FRANK: I fancied myself a sort of ambassador. Me, inviting all of you into my world. That's why I wore a suit. Ambassadors need to make a good impression.

FRANCES: But you're not wearing a suit right now.

FRANK: I'm not. But that was the day I decided to dress up my thoughts too. Even if I'm not wearing a suit, my brain is always wearing a tuxedo. Do you see?

FRANCES: The tuxedo?

FRANK: No. Not just the tuxedo. *(Pause.)* Look at Milly. Milly's got to primp her brain too. Like if she's got an evening gown on her mind *(Frank takes a moment to visualize this.)*, we can imagine the courtship of our two thoughts.

MILLY: The end of the maze.

FRANK: Like those little rodents that sneak their heads out of the ground and look around. *(To Frances.)* That's how I felt before I met your sister. There was always dirt in my eyes.

MILLY: Exactly. That's what I'm saying, Frances.

FRANK: The problem is, you're looking at the world as if there was some answer.

FRANCES: I'm not looking for answers.

MILLY: There's nothing wrong with looking for answers.

FRANCES: Actually I'm not. Really. I might have been before but I'm here now and I think I understand and I'm not.

FRANK: But you're looking for something so look at the two of us as an example. I spent my entire life looking for something, and when I realized it didn't exist I was a much happier person.

MILLY: *(Pause.)* Thanks.

FRANK: No, thank you, honey.

FRANCES: *(To Milly.)* We shouldn't talk about this anymore.

FRANK: But we haven't gotten to the beauty; the beauty of giving over. You just accept that no one is you. You see? And once you do that, you can accept that no one is right for you. And then, then you can finally settle down into the living. *(Looking around the living room.)* Settling into this room for example... Settling in all ways. *(Pause.)* I could go for a Hot Toddy right now. Milly? *(Pause.)* All right. *(Frank goes to make a drink. The three sit in silence. Frank mumbles.)* Put on the tuxedo, Frank! Time to put on that tuxedo. *(To Milly.)* Thinking out loud again. Milly, you caught me thinking out loud again.

FRANCES: Thinking what?

FRANK: Just thinking that you shouldn't worry about it, Frances.

FRANCES: Right.

FRANK: Right, Milly?

   (Milly stares at Frank.)

MILLY: Right, Frank.

   (Milly gets up and exits. Frank looks at the door, waiting for Milly's return. A long pause.)

FRANK: Right.

   (Frances and Frank sit silent in the living room. The lights fade.)

END OF PLAY

Lunchtime
by Rob Marcato

CHARACTERS

ANGELA: Approaching thirty.
DONNA: Early to mid-twenties.
MAN

SETTING

A food court or public cafeteria at lunchtime in the business district of a major city.

Lunchtime

A food court or large, public cafeteria—the seating area of small tables and chairs. It's lunch hour in the business district of a major city.

Angela and Donna are about halfway through lunch. The cafeteria is moderately crowded at this hour, but they are in their usual corner, which is relatively empty. They sit at a small table. Two or more tables are on stage but empty. The two women are dressed nicely, in office attire. Angela clearly spends time on her looks (hair, make-up, clothes). Donna spends less, but is pretty in her own natural way.

The lights come up. After a short silence, Donna speaks.

DONNA: So, should I ask about last night or—

ANGELA: Oh God, please don't. *(Pause.)* You know, it wouldn't bother me half as much if he gave me a reason. You know, like "I'm coming off a painful breakup and I don't want to rush into things" or "I've had a perpetual headache for the past month" or "My sister has a schnauzer that's more attractive than you"—

DONNA: Angela.

ANGELA: No, I know. *(Beat.)* And you know me, I'm all for taking things slow. In fact, I'm usually on the other side of this. But this isn't taking it slow. We're not moving. We're in "park."

DONNA: What happened?

ANGELA: What happened? What always happens. He came over. I cooked for him. I mean, I *cooked* for him—an indication of the depths of desperation to which I have sunk. We ate, we talked. We sat on my couch, we talked. It was lovely. A bottle of wine was consumed, mostly by me. I'm sending him signals strong enough to attract a small army. Then, all of a sudden it's "I've had a wonderful time, but I have to get up for work tomorrow," as if I don't, a kiss on the forehead and out the door.

DONNA: I'm sorry.

ANGELA: Oh God, then this morning—

DONNA: I heard.

ANGELA: Fucking Meyerson stomps in after his nine o'clock presentation, which apparently did not go too well, because he's ranting and raving that I didn't do the margins and spacing the way he asked for them, which of course I did, like bigger margins are gonna hide the fact that he's a clueless schmuck. *(Beat.)* So, naturally, I've been a powerhouse bitch to everyone this morning. And now you're stuck listening to me bitch about it.

DONNA: No, that's what I'm here for. If you can't bitch to me, who can you bitch to.

ANGELA: Well, thank you, but I don't know how you put up with me.

DONNA: *(Beat.)* I sorta tune you out and just smile and nod my head a lot.
(Donna smiles.)

ANGELA: *(Looks up surprised. Then, laughing.)* That was good. I'm proud of you.

DONNA: Thanks. *(Beat.)* One good thing about today though. Your little friend isn't here.

ANGELA: I was about to say. It looks like he won't be joining us today. Maybe I should ask *him* out. At least I know he'd *listen* to me. Though, I think *you're* the one he's got a thing for.

DONNA: Don't even joke about that.
(They laugh. Pause. Then, Angela notices Man coming toward them, but offstage.)

ANGELA: Oh, see now, we had to go and talk about him. We couldn't leave well enough alone.

DONNA: What, is he here?

ANGELA: Uh huh.
(Man enters, stops, and looks over the available tables. He is dressed plainly, in a button-down shirt and slacks. He holds a tray of food, with a newspaper tucked under his arm. The following narration pretty closely matches Man's actions.)

ANGELA: Hmmm. Now, let's see. Where ever shall I sit today? Oh, lookey there. Out of all these tables, why don't I choose the one right next to those two women over there, so I can inconspicuously eavesdrop on their conversation. *(Man moves to a table behind Donna and sits in its only chair, with his back to the women. Then, he remembers something and stands.)* Oh! I mustn't forget the extra chair for my imaginary friend who will never join me.
(He takes a chair from a nearby table, places it across from his, then sits again and begins eating and reading. Angela and Donna talk in low voices.)

DONNA: He'll hear you.

ANGELA: Well, that's what he wants, isn't it?

DONNA: Do you really think he…

ANGELA: Oh, come on. Once is a fluke, twice is a coincidence, but this is getting ridiculous.

DONNA: Okay, I'll admit he sits next to us a lot, but that doesn't mean he's listening to us.

ANGELA: Then what's he doing—enjoying our perfume?

DONNA: I don't know. I just think we're being a little paranoid. He seems pretty harmless to me.

ANGELA: My lovely, charming, naïve, trusting friend. You are a stalker's dream. *(Beat.)* Am I gonna have to prove this to you? *(Beat.)* Here. Watch him.

DONNA: What?

ANGELA: *(Motioning for Donna to turn toward Man.)* Watch him. *(Donna covertly looks at him. Then, in a louder voice.)* So I heard this great new joke this morning. What's the difference between a lightbulb and a pregnant woman?

DONNA: *(Beat. Then, realizing it's her cue.)* Oh, uh, what?

ANGELA: You can't unscrew a pregnant woman. *(Both Donna and Angela laugh. Man laughs silently so that his shoulders shake slightly.)* Did you see that?

DONNA: What?

ANGELA: His shoulders shook. *(Beat.)* He was laughing. His little, narrow shoulders shook, and so did his hand and the paper.

DONNA: Maybe a little. You did say it pretty loud, though.

ANGELA: Oh, come on. He was listening to us.

DONNA: Okay, fine. So let's say he's listening to us.

ANGELA: He is.

DONNA: Okay. So, what can we do about it? Do you want to move?

ANGELA: No. We shouldn't have to move. This is our table. We sit here every day.

DONNA: Well, I agree. But, I mean, what can we do about it then?

ANGELA: *(Beat.)* I'm gonna say something to him.

DONNA: What?

ANGELA: I'm gonna tell the fucker not to sit here anymore.

DONNA: Angela.

ANGELA: *(To Man.)* Excuse me.

DONNA: Angela.

ANGELA: Excuse me. *(Man turns to face them, and Donna looks down at her lap, embarrassed.)* Hi. Um…my friend and I were wondering if you could… you know, sit someplace else.

MAN: Excuse me?

ANGELA: You know. Sit…not near us.

MAN: I'm sorry, I don't … I don't think I—

ANGELA: Oh, come on. I'm sure you don't mean any harm, but we know what you're doing.

MAN: What I'm… I don't understand what—

ANGELA: You know—listening.

MAN: *(Beat.)* Well, I don't know what you're implying, but I certainly—

ANGELA: *(Forcefully.)* Okay, stop playing dumb. Could you please go sit somewhere else.

MAN: *(Beat.)* Listen, I don't know what I did to you, but… This is my seat. I have a right to sit here. You can… I have a right to sit here.

(Man turns back to his paper.)

ANGELA: *(She stares at him in frustration and disbelief. Then, throwing in the towel.)* Okay, fine. You win. Sit there. Listen to our conversation. *(Under her breath.)* Fuckin' stalker.

(Man hears this, and is clearly unsettled by it. He turns to Angela.)

MAN: *(Timid, but angry.)* You're very rude.

(Back to his paper.)

ANGELA: *(Looking up.)* Excuse me?

DONNA: Angela.

ANGELA: Hey! I'm rude? I'm "very rude"? What, eavesdropping on other people's conversations doesn't qualify as rude?

MAN: *(Looking up, adamant.)* I don't … I don't do that.

ANGELA: Oh, you don't, do you? *(She walks quickly to him, snatches the paper out of his hands, and moves to the other side of his table.)* Okay. Then tell me something from today's news.

MAN: Could you please give me my paper back?

ANGELA: Come on. Just one story. One headline. One picture. Tell me one thing you perused while you weren't desperately trying to hear every word we said.

MAN: I… I don't have to… Could you please—

ANGELA: You can't, can you? No. But I bet you can tell me the difference between a lightbulb and a pregnant woman, can't you?

MAN: Listen. Could you please leave me alone?

ANGELA: Oh, I'm sorry. Am I sitting in someone's seat?

MAN: Well…yes.

ANGELA: Who are you waiting for? A ladyfriend?

MAN: That's none of your business.

ANGELA: Ooooh, a ladyfriend. I'd love to meet her. I think I'll just stay here until she comes.

MAN: Why are you doing this to me? I haven't done anything to you.

ANGELA: You sit here every day and listen to our conversations. Don't you see anything wrong with that?

MAN: I haven't hurt you, have I?

ANGELA: These are *our* conversations—the intimate details of *our* lives. They are not for *you*. Go find your own.

(Angela starts to return to her table.)

MAN: You are cruel.

(Angela stops.)

ANGELA: *(Hands on the back of the empty chair.)* At least I don't have to eat alone.

MAN: You are a cruel person.

ANGELA: *(Pushing the chair until it hits the table.)* At least I'm not waiting for imaginary friends.

MAN: *(A warning.)* Don't push me.

ANGELA: *(Pushing the chair and table into him.)* Friends that will never fucking come!

MAN: *(Beat. Then, awkwardly, but with real venom.)* I wish your boyfriend would just fuck you and get it over with so you could stop taking your frustrations out on other people. If only he could get it up with you in the room. Have you tried putting a bag over your head? That might help.

(Pause. Angela is stunned at first. Then, shock turns to fury.)

ANGELA: You son of a bitch!

(Angela runs at him and falls onto him, beating him with flailing arms. He curls into a ball with his hands on top of his head, repeating "I'm sorry" over and over again. Donna goes to them and does her best to pull Angela off him. She is able to do so. Angela stands for a moment, stunned, then runs offstage. Donna watches her exit, looks back over the room, also stunned, then starts after Angela. Man moans in pain, holding his hands to his forehead. Donna hears him, stops, and turns to look at him.)

DONNA: *(Beat.)* Are you okay?

MAN: It's only a scratch, I think.

DONNA: Let me see.

(Man gingerly removes his hands from his forehead. From a few feet away, Donna examines it. There is a large, red scratch on his forehead.)

DONNA: Ooh, she really got you there.

MAN: She has long nails.

(Donna deliberates for a moment, looks offstage where Angela exited, then back at Man.)

DONNA: Here. *(She takes a napkin from her table and dips it in her water. Then, moving tentatively to him, she cleans the scratch with the napkin and presses on it.)* I'm really sorry about that.

MAN: It's not your fault. You're very kind. *(Beat.)* Why are you friends with her?

DONNA: Oh. She's not all bad. I mean, she's had a rough life, but she's got a big heart and she's very good to me.

MAN: I love that about you. No matter what, you always manage to see the good in people.

(Donna steps back from him.)

DONNA: I really should go make sure she's okay.

(Donna starts to leave.)

MAN: Donna! *(She turns to him.)* Uh... I was just wondering if...you know, sometime you might want to...or if you and I could ... I was just—

DONNA: Are you asking me out?

MAN: *(Desperately explaining.)* It wasn't supposed to be like that. I mean, I'm not supposed to be like that. I'm not like that, or at least I haven't been for a long time.

DONNA: You just insulted my friend, and now you're asking me out?

(Donna rushes to pick up her bag and Angela's.)

MAN: Listen, I don't care about her, I care about you. I would never do that to you. *(As Donna exits.)* I would never hurt you.

(Man is left alone. Lights down.)

END OF PLAY

The Hour of Lamps
by Debbie Mitchell

CHARACTERS

CELIA: An author of children's books.

KEVIN: Her younger brother.

ROSE: Older sister to both Kevin and Celia.

PLACE

Celia's studio apartment.

TIME

The present, a rainy evening in early summer.

The Hour of Lamps

The opening monologue is spoken by Celia, who is seated at a writing desk in a sparsely furnished apartment. As she speaks, the figure of a young man, dimly lit, appears behind her. He gives the impression of a sleepwalker—walking through an imaginary field of tall grass; he goes through the motions of catching lightning bugs and placing them in a Jif peanut butter jar with holes punched through the top.

Music up. A soft haunting piano melody, something like Elmer Bernstein's score for To Kill a Mockingbird.

CELIA: To my eyes my brother has not changed since childhood. He is an elf of twenty-six, skipping over endless summer lawns, his shirttails swinging over his bell-bottomed jeans—wearing an incandescent yellow rain slicker like Mama used to buy for him at K-Mart. From behind he looks like an empty overcoat—straying and bewitched. He has deliberately chosen his tedious day job because it keeps locked in a cubicle that part of himself that looks deceptively like a man. The rest of him is free to sing, compose and fly back to the past, to rejoin the boy of six who opened every watch, collected epitaphs, and played the piano from birth. He finds him again without difficulty...slips into the light little body that he never leaves for long, and roams through a country of the mind where all is to the liking of one who has triumphantly remained a child. But no child is invulnerable, and this one sometimes comes back to me, badly hurt because he has tried to confront his well-remembered dream with a reality that betrays it. *(A knock.)*

CELIA: Come on in. It's open.

KEVIN: Celia, Snow White Sister! Look what I bring you. Treasures of the night, surpassing the plain gems of the earth! I slid up the slender wand of light from the North Star and peeled the Pleiades off their black velvet evening capes. *(He offers her the lightning-bug jar.)*

CELIA: All right, all right, enough verbiage! You still use too many adjectives. *(Hugs him.)* But I'm so glad to see you. *(Picking up the jar.)* Aren't they beautiful? I used to love to wear lightning-bug stingers around my wrist on hot summer nights. They always looked so cool…reminded me of the beaded neck of the water cooler in the public library. Thank you, Kevin.

KEVIN: *(Hugging her again, a little too tightly.)* Is it safe? Is Rose here?

CELIA: Now don't be mean to her. She's your big sister, too, and she's worried about you.

KEVIN: Hey! Do you have something to eat around here? You know what I could REALLY go for? Some Peeps!

CELIA: PEEPS?

KEVIN: Yeah, Peeps. Those marshmallow bunnies and chickens with the pink and yellow poster paint color coats.

CELIA: Oh God! Those things are disgusting. Besides don't they only sell them at Walgreen's, shrouded in ritual? At the spring equinox?

KEVIN: Naw, naw. They're just getting RIPE. The BEST time to buy them is a couple weeks after Easter when they're about ninety-nine cents for 500. Then you put them in your winter coat pockets.

CELIA: *(Laughing.)* OOOOOOO! Gross!

KEVIN: It's a delicacy!

ROSE: *(Enters from offstage, the kitchen.)* Still taking good care of your health, I see.

KEVIN: Aww now, Rose—

ROSE: We have some leftover steamed vegetables on the stove. They're still warm. I'll get some for you. *(She exits to kitchen.)*

KEVIN: No, no. If you REALLY don't have any Peeps, then I'd just like a peanut butter and jelly sandwich—*(Yelling after her.)* WITH CRUNCHED-UP POTATO CHIPS ON TOP.

ROSE: *(Yelling from offstage, pretending not to hear him.)* Or we have some cracked wheat and stuffed peppers.

KEVIN: How about a giant pixie stick… GRAPE?

ROSE: *(Reentering. The barter has turned serious. She speaks deliberately to him.)* Would you like a tuna sandwich on wheat bread?

KEVIN: *(Grinning.)* Betty Crocker vanilla frosting on graham crackers?

ROSE: *(Relenting a little, hopefully.)* Granola?

KEVIN: Sold. Actually raisins only. Would you get me a little box of Sun-Maid raisins? I'll just eat them out of the box. And take your time.
(Rose exits.)

KEVIN: Celia—*(He starts to speak further to her but is cut off by a voice, again from the kitchen.)*

ROSE: How's your songwriting going? Have you had time to practice your piano?

KEVIN: *(Obviously lying.)* Yeah. I have been doing…that. A lot. *(Pause, desperately.)* Really!

ROSE: *(Entering with a bowl of granola.)* Kevin, you should NOT neglect such an extraordinary gift. I mean it. You're too talented to—

KEVIN: Rose Red Sister, stop talking a minute and just let me look at you…at both my sisters. There stand together, that's good. You look to me just like you did in grade school, pausing on the pavement, a pair of cotton sundresses with green buttons, looking as bright as a pair of Mama's tea roses. Remember? At the old house—?

ROSE: *(Unimpressed by his usual purple prose.)* Kevin—are you still seeing your therapist?

KEVIN: Uh…well, now about that, I had a few problems… *(Beginning to perform a little premeditated comic piece designed for this question.)* First of all, YOU *(Pointing to Rose.)* called him and told him I was forgetting to breathe, or something weird like that. He was convinced I needed to CONFRONT someone or other. So, I was supposed to pretend the person I needed to confront was sitting in the next chair, but the thing was I had to SWITCH CHAIRS to answer as I thought THEY would answer. I said, "Can't I just sit HERE and answer for them?" Oh noo, that was not acceptable. So I switched back and forth, back and forth, until he smiled smugly and said, "See, you're getting short of breath." I said, "I'm EXHAUSTED." He just could NOT conceive that I could do both characters from the same chair.

(Celia laughs at his performance.)

ROSE: Oh, that's a good reason for quitting therapy.

KEVIN: He has no imagination. He couldn't even understand why the song "Good Bye Ol' Paint" is so terribly sad. He looked at me like I was crazy when I told him about sitting in the back of elementary music with Miss Pometere— *(To Celia.)* remember, who always had that little bit of red lipstick on her front tooth?—and just crying through the whole cowboy unit.

ROSE: Find someone else then. Why don't you grow up just a LITTLE bit? Do you want to be like this at forty? At sixty? What is so great about childhood anyway? I HATED IT! I couldn't wait to leave those preadolescent wildcats who ripped the heart out of anything that was different from them. I couldn't WAIT to leave lime-green concrete walls and the smell of Salisbury steak! You could let your music help you out, but you've left it completely behind, and all you've got left is nostalgia—a stiff white meringue shell with absolutely NO TASTE AT ALL! WHY?

CELIA: Rose, stop. You know this doesn't help.

ROSE: Why do you do this to yourself? You're such a waste and…a COWARD.

KEVIN: *(Sputtering for words.)* And you're a…a COSMIC DO-OVER!

ROSE: A WHAT?

KEVIN: A DO-OVER! You know, like in kickball—only on a universal scale. You should have to go back to home base and do your childhood over!

ROSE: OOOOOOOO! Stop reducing my anger to your playground terms!

KEVIN: I mean it. You need to live life over to appreciate the beauty you missed. You call your escapism dedication, and society accepts that. So you're a big success on your way to Germany with an unpronounceable opera company. Well I don't WANT to settle into what society calls adult responsibilities. But things keep changing, and every day the child in me fights harder to survive. I'm not aging gracefully. The process is sloppy. But I'd rather be in my messed-up memory world—I'd rather see fresh white sheets of sunlight on the first morning of summer vacation, than the cold white spotlight eyes that follow you. I'd rather see August storm clouds made blacker by porch screens than YOUR lonely, empty black rooms—away from your family most of your life—Why don't you go! You MUST have some rehearsal to go to. Go ahead and "transcend your past." PLEASE transcend me at least and GET OUT!

ROSE: At least I can touch and smell the things in my world RIGHT NOW— it has a current and beautiful sound. Time is sucking away the tangibles from yours. I know you, Kevin. You CAN'T live completely in your memory. You need to be touched. All of your senses are becoming embalmed. I'm afraid you'll die with them. Please, PLEASE let in some new life. That's all.

(Rose stares at him steadily, picks up her music by the door, and leaves.)

CELIA: *(Crosses to Rose, smooths her hair gently, and kisses her cheek.)* I'll call you later. *(To Kevin.)* We haven't been together in weeks. Did you have to—

KEVIN: *(Cutting her off.)* Yes. I had to.

(Celia retreats to her writing desk. Kevin begins to play with a waistcoat watch in his pocket.)

KEVIN: Celia?

CELIA: Yes?

KEVIN: I've been BACK THERE. Did you know?

CELIA: *(Envious.)* You've been back to Webster Groves? How?

KEVIN: I told them at work there was a death in the family. I rode back with a girl from the office. I couldn't resist. It was such a beautiful day—a hot still afternoon when everything was asleep, even the water in the gutters.

CELIA: How was it? Tell me everything!

KEVIN: It was...all right. *(He relapses into silence, staring at the lightning-bug jar and whistling to himself. Celia decides to wait him out.)* Celia? Back THERE I went to the old house on Blue Lake.

CELIA: Oh! I haven't been there in years. How does it look? Is Mama's garden still there? And the woods we called our enchanted forest?

KEVIN: Gone. Cut down. Nothing left. A clean sweep. You can see the earth. You can see... *(Swipes the air with his hand.)* ...and that's not all. I walked down to the Revolutionary Heroes Graveyard. My favorite, my very favorite place, remember?

CELIA: And?

KEVIN: No wait. I have to tell it from the beginning. I am sitting on the porch of the old house. It's cool and melancholy on the front steps. The smell of crushed grass hangs over the unmown lawn, and I'm just sitting there listening to breakers of locusts and the low rumble of airplanes... That SOUND... I can't describe how peaceful. I begin to walk slowly, rhythmically, on the downbeat of the cricket. It's the time Mama always called the hour of lamps, that most strange and mysterious time in a neighborhood, when everything that was green a moment ago is now blue, and I find myself at the lower entrance to the graveyard—the one near Mrs. Downs.

CELIA: Not Mrs. Downs. She must have been dead for years now.

KEVIN: Maybe. I don't know. I guess they did give me another name, but if THEY think I'm going to remember a name, I don't know! Well ... I go in through the lower entrance. *(Irritably.)* Come to think of it, the dogs didn't even bark when I pushed the door open.

CELIA: *(Gently.)* Come on Kev, there couldn't have been the same dogs. Just think about it.

KEVIN: Okay, it's a minor detail, I won't even mention the Astroturf they've put over Mrs. Downs' verandah. *(He pauses.)*

CELIA: And was that all?

KEVIN: No. As I started up toward the creek that runs toward the graveyard gate, if you could call that filthy cesspool a creek, but never mind, I really didn't pay that much attention to it—because I was waiting for the moment of the gate.

CELIA: What moment of the gate?

KEVIN: Come on! Can't you see the knob of the gate?

CELIA: Yes, yes… I can see it. Shiny, black cast iron…as though I could reach out and touch it.

KEVIN: Well as long as I've known it, when you turn it like this *(Mimics opening the gate.)* and let go of the gate, it opens through its own weight, and as it swings it says:

BOTH: *(In unison.)* EEE-EE-EEE-AAAY!

KEVIN: *(Frantically.)* That's right! I turned it. I let the gate go. I listened. Do you know what THEY'VE done?

CELIA: No.

KEVIN: THEY'VE OILED THE GATE!

(Lights dim. Celia appears in spotlight at her table. Kevin picks up the lightning-bug jar and walks, trancelike, away. The haunting piano theme returns.)

CELIA: He left almost immediately. I didn't even have a chance to speak. He wrapped himself in the damp membrane of the raincoat and walked away poorer by four notes. I watched him from my window. The insects' green and yellow lights looked fuzzy in the fine rain that was falling. Then—in the wink of a street lamp—I saw an emerald comet split the sky and explode on the wet pavement in a single broken glass chord. In the summer that was to follow, Kevin wore his shirttails tucked in—most of the time…but on certain midsummer nights I would see him, cross-legged on the grass, his musician's ear straining to catch that most delicate of offertories composed by an ancient gate, a grain of sand, a trace of rust—and dedicated to the one untamed child who was worthy of it.

(Blackout. Music fade out.)

END OF PLAY

The Sin-Eater
by Don Nigro

CHARACTERS

THE SIN-EATER: A ragged young man.
THE ELDER SISTER: Dressed in black.
THE YOUNGER SISTER: Dressed in white.

SETTING

A room in a house in Wales in another time, and the shore by the mill race, downstage at the edge of the light. In the room is a bed and three wooden chairs.

Sin-Eater: a person who in former times in certain parts of Wales, Scotland, and England would through a ritual devouring of food and drink take upon himself the sins of the deceased. The food was often placed on the chest of the corpse. After the meal had been devoured, the sin-eater was driven from the house amid a hail of thrown objects and execrations.

The Sin-Eater

Lights up on a bed and three wooden chairs on an otherwise dark stage. A small house in Wales in another time. The Elder Sister stands at the foot of the bed, in quiet mourning. The Younger Sister lies still in the bed. The Sin-Eater, a poor young man, watches them.

THE SIN-EATER: My job always. Mother was before me. Someone must do it, she said, and we have been chosen. It is a dark privilege only we can acknowledge, she said. Their contempt is our badge of honor. We are the closest, she said, to understanding the mystery of Christ on earth. Like him, we are the sin-eaters. Live in a shack at the edge of the village. Shunned by all until their time of need. Someone dies, then I am summoned. But this time it was a different thing. Oh, Jesus help me. This time it was a different matter entirely. They were two sisters, I had watched them since they were little girls, the elder dark and quiet, the younger bright and lively, and both so beautiful, their eyes and their hair, to see them walk down green paths in spring, at water's edge in summer, through red and gold woods in autumn, on ice in winter, oh, those two, always together, always so lovely, the elder quiet, watching, the younger laughing, teasing the boys. The elder now and then took pity on me, brought me food, left it at the gate for me, but the younger threw rocks and called me names and laughed. I loved the younger. I loved the spirit of life in her. It is true she ripped my heart out with her hands on all occasions, and made jokes at my expense, but still I loved her and could think no harm of her. Then came word I was wanted at their house. I hoped at first it was another cruel joke, but no. The younger had died suddenly. She lay dead now in her bed. I must come and do what only I could do. Oh, God, oh, God this is a more exquisite punishment and torment than ever you have given me. To enter that house. I have dreamed of that house. In my dreams I have walked in that house, and come to that bed, and crept into it with my beloved. Now I must enter it and eat her sins from off her breast.

THE ELDER SISTER: Well, what are you gawking at? Come here, boy. What is wrong with you?

THE SIN-EATER: I'm sorry. I just—I'm sorry.

THE ELDER SISTER: You act as if you've never done this before.

THE SIN-EATER: I've done this many times.

THE ELDER SISTER: Then why do you hang back like a guilty dog? She is dead, boy. She can throw no more rocks at you now. Do you think to take your revenge upon her by refusing to eat her sins?

THE SIN-EATER: Revenge?

THE ELDER SISTER: I know that she was cruel to you and did torment you. I am sorry for that. She meant no harm, I swear to you, she did not. She had such life in her, it must be bursting out in all directions. She had all the world in her. Every grief and joy, every love and hate—no, not hate, there was no hate in her, there was anger, and impatience, and perhaps now and then a cruel sense of humor, but she was gentle and loving, all animals loved her, and all souls on earth, but you, perhaps. You must not blame her for being young and sometimes thoughtless. She was a good girl and meant no evil.

THE SIN-EATER: I never blamed your sister. She was welcome to throw rocks at me. I took great pleasure knowing that she lived. I grieve for her as you do.

THE ELDER SISTER: That is a very Christian thing.

THE SIN-EATER: No.

THE ELDER SISTER: Watch over her while I get the food.

THE SIN-EATER: Yes. I will watch over her. (*The Elder Sister looks at the corpse for a moment, then goes. He approaches the bed shyly.*) Oh, God. She is still ungodly beautiful. Even in death she seems to live. I cannot bear to think of her sweet body rotting in the earth. Jesus, Jesus.
(*He falls to his knees and rests his forehead against the foot of the bed.*)

THE YOUNGER SISTER: (*Lying motionless on the bed.*) The problem is, I'm not dead. I mean, it would seem that I am dead, but the fact is, I can hear everything they say, I can hear the owls out my window, I can smell the flowers in my room, I have heard my sister sobbing over me, I felt her tenderly bathe my corpse, which was not at all an unpleasant sensation, except that I wanted to tell her I'm not dead, only I could not speak, I could not move, I could not even open my eyes, and yet my heart beats, slowly, slowly, but it beats, I want to scream at her that I am alive, but nothing comes out. It is some sort of epileptic fit, it must be, I remember our mother telling me once that our grandfather used to have these, that once he interrupted his own funeral by sitting up and announcing that he wanted some crackers. How can I let them know I'm alive? Perhaps I can pee. Let me try. Ooooo. Ooooo. Alas, nothing. Not a drop. If only I'd had that extra cup of tea before my unfortunate demise. Oh, dear. What if they bury me? What if they bury me? Hello. I'm in here. Please don't bury me. Oh, why can't they hear me? And what is that loathsome boy doing with his head at my feet? I wish he would keep away from my feet.

THE ELDER SISTER: *(Returning with a plate upon which are placed bread, cheese, and wine.)* What are you doing?

THE SIN-EATER: Praying for her soul.

THE ELDER SISTER: It is not the job of the sin-eater to pray. It is the job of the sin-eater to eat the sins of the dead, and thus take them upon himself. Here is the food. *(She puts the plate on the Younger Sister's chest.)* Are you ready? You don't look well, boy.

THE SIN-EATER: I don't know if I can do this.

THE ELDER SISTER: Of course you can do this. Why couldn't you do this? This is what you do. This is how you make your living, such as it is. If you don't eat my sister's sins from off her breast, who will? You are the only sin-eater in the village. What is it? Do you want more money?

THE SIN-EATER: No, no, it isn't the money. It's her.

THE ELDER SISTER: What's wrong with her?

THE SIN-EATER: Nothing. Nothing is wrong with her.

THE YOUNGER SISTER: I'm not dead, that's what's wrong with me.

THE ELDER SISTER: Then do your work and be done with it. There is bread and cheese and wine. Do you need anything else?

THE YOUNGER SISTER: I'd like some crackers.

THE SIN-EATER: No. This will be fine.

THE ELDER SISTER: I will be just in the next room. Let me know when you're done.

THE SIN-EATER: Yes. I will.

THE ELDER SISTER: I still can't believe she's dead.

THE YOUNGER SISTER: Me neither.

THE ELDER SISTER: She looks so lovely there.

THE SIN-EATER: Yes.

THE ELDER SISTER: Well. I'll go then. Don't take forever.

THE YOUNGER SISTER: Don't go. Don't leave me alone with this revolting person. I'm not dead. I'm not dead. Look, I'm attempting to pee.

(The Elder Sister goes. The Sin-Eater looks at the body.)

THE SIN-EATER: So sweet she looks. So innocent.

THE YOUNGER SISTER: I'm not dead, you simpleton. Can't you tell I'm breathing, you great, foul-smelling ignoramus?

THE SIN-EATER: I must eat her sins now. I must eat her sins. This is the one thing I can do for her. This is the only act of love which is permitted of me. I will never love another. I have only loved her. I will only love her. She is all the world to me. And now she lies here dead before me on her bed.

THE YOUNGER SISTER: I'm alive, you jackass. You blockhead. You lip-diddling imbecile. Can't you see that I'm alive? Get this crap off my chest and get away from me. You smell like a small animal has died in your pants.

THE SIN-EATER: I'm not hungry.

THE YOUNGER SISTER: Well, I am. I'm starving to death. Could I have a piece of that cheese if you don't want it?

THE SIN-EATER: I am so unhappy, I cannot eat.

THE YOUNGER SISTER: I can eat. I can eat. Just give me a drink of wine, why don't you? Listen to me, bean head. Hello? Hello? An important message for the village idiot. Your beloved is not yet ready for the maggot farm. Hello?

THE SIN-EATER: Oh, God. I am having evil thoughts. I am having evil thoughts.

THE YOUNGER SISTER: Uh oh. I don't like the sound of that.

THE SIN-EATER: I must resist these evil thoughts. But I have loved her for so long. And now, to be alone with her, here in her bedroom—

THE YOUNGER SISTER: Help. Somebody help. Necrophilia. Necrophilia.

THE SIN-EATER: I have dreamed so often of this moment. Except of course she was not dead. Sleeping, perhaps. Oh, I must kiss her. Just once, just once before they put her in the cold earth, I must kiss her perfect lips.

THE YOUNGER SISTER: He is not going to kiss me. He is not going to kiss me.

THE SIN-EATER: I am going to kiss her.

THE YOUNGER SISTER: He is going to kiss me. He is going to kiss me. Now I wish I really was dead. Oh, oh, this is disgusting. This is disgusting. This—*(The Sin-Eater very tenderly and reverently puts his lips to hers and kisses her, a long, long, very sensual kiss. Then he pulls back.)* Jesus, James, and Mary.

THE SIN-EATER: Oh, God.

THE YOUNGER SISTER: Oh, God.

THE SIN-EATER: *This is a terrible thing, what I've done. This is a terrible, terrible thing.*

THE YOUNGER SISTER: A terrible thing. Do it again.

THE SIN-EATER: And what's even worse, I'm going to do it again.

THE YOUNGER SISTER: Oh, good, he's going to do it again. He's going to do it again.

(He kisses her again, long, reverential, and very erotic. In the middle of this the Elder Sister returns, sees them.)

THE ELDER SISTER: Just what the devil do you think you're doing?

THE SIN-EATER: *(Jumping away from the body.)* Ahhhh. Oh, I was just, I was— it's part of the ritual, we—

THE ELDER SISTER: Get the hell away from my sister. You despicable, monstrous creature. Get away from her. Get out. Get out of here. Get out. *(She is pulling him away, beating and kicking him.)* Out. Get out. Vermin. Excrement.

THE SIN-EATER: But I love her. I love her.

THE ELDER SISTER: I will tell the men of the village, and they will tear you to pieces, you vicious, evil, filthy, filthy man. Get. Get out. Get out.

(She chases him away. He moves downstage and sits on the ground at the edge of the light, in despair.)

THE YOUNGER SISTER: *(Sitting up in bed.)* Oh, no, you mustn't be mean to him.

THE ELDER SISTER: Mean to him? I'll be mean to him if I please. Do you know what that son of a— *(She looks at the Younger Sister, sees her sitting up.)* AHHHHHHHHHHHHHH.

THE YOUNGER SISTER: AHHHHHHH. Don't shriek at me like that. Do you want to kill me all over again?

THE ELDER SISTER: What is happening here? Am I going mad? Have you come back from the dead?

THE YOUNGER SISTER: I was sleeping. Don't you remember about Grandpa and the crackers? Which reminds me, God I'm hungry. What have we got to eat around here? *(Grabbing the plate with the Sin-Eater's food on it.)* Oh, this looks good.

(The Younger Sister begins to eat.)

THE ELDER SISTER: I don't understand this. I don't understand this at all. We had already dug the hole in the backyard.

THE YOUNGER SISTER: Maybe we can plant some azaleas. Now, run and get me some more food. Hurry. And bring back the Sin-Eater.

THE ELDER SISTER: You don't want to see that wretched man. He tried to molest you while you were dead.

THE YOUNGER SISTER: *(Chomping on the bread.)* He kissed me. He brought me back to life. It was incredible. My toes are still tingling. Go and get him. I want to see him. Now. Or I might drop dead again.

THE ELDER SISTER: All right, all right.

(The Elder Sister runs out.)

THE YOUNGER SISTER: *(Sitting on the bed and eating, yelling after her sister.)* DO WE HAVE ANY LAMB CHOPS?

THE SIN-EATER: I've kissed the dead lips of my beloved. Nothing else matters now. The men of the village will come and tear me to pieces. I don't mind. I would rather be dead with her. I think I will just lie down here in the water. Yes, I will just lie down here and remember her kiss and let the water creep up over my head.

(He lies down on the stage, as if lying back in water, and is still.)

THE YOUNGER SISTER: FOOD. I WANT MORE FOOD. AND WHAT THE HELL KIND OF CHEESE IS THIS? IT TASTES LIKE FUNGUS.

THE ELDER SISTER: *(Returning with a plate of food.)* This is all we have left in the house.

THE YOUNGER SISTER: Great. Where is my Sin-Eater? I want my Sin-Eater.

THE ELDER SISTER: Listen, dear. I have some bad news for you, but I hope it will not spoil your resurrection. The Sin-Eater has drowned himself in the mill race. They have laid his body out there on the shore.

THE YOUNGER SISTER: He's dead? The Sin-Eater is dead? Are you sure? Couldn't he be sleeping just as I was? Couldn't it be like Grandpa and the crackers? Maybe it's contagious.

THE ELDER SISTER: No, dear. I am sorry. He is drowned.

THE YOUNGER SISTER: Oh. Oh, no.

THE ELDER SISTER: Here. Have some more food.

THE YOUNGER SISTER: I have lost my appetite entirely. Why would he drown himself?

THE ELDER SISTER: It must have been guilt for kissing your corpse. He didn't know you only slept.

THE YOUNGER SISTER: Oh, poor boy. Poor lonely creature. He never knew. He saved me and he never knew. And what about his sins? Who will eat his sins for him? There is no sin-eater to eat his sins. He has died with his sins upon him, and all the sins he has eaten, and there is no one to eat his sins. I must go to him.

THE ELDER SISTER: You're not strong enough. You've just got over being dead.

THE YOUNGER SISTER: I must go to him now. He needs me.

THE ELDER SISTER: What could he need you for? The man is dead.

THE YOUNGER SISTER: I must eat his sins.

THE ELDER SISTER: You cannot eat his sins. You'll be shunned as he was. They will throw stones at you and spit at you.

THE YOUNGER SISTER: I don't care. I don't care. I must eat his sins. Someone must eat his sins. He gave me life, and I must eat his sins. *(She takes the new plate of food and goes to the edge of the light where the Sin-Eater lies still.)* Hello. I've brought you some food. Here. *(She carefully puts the plate of food on his chest.)* I'm going to eat your sins now. I think it's only right. I don't care if they shun me, if they throw rocks and jeer at me and spit at me. You kissed me. You gave me life. I want to do this thing. This is what love is, I think. The eating of the other's sins. And yet I have no appetite. You are really quite beautiful, you know. *(Pause. She looks at him.)* Perhaps just one kiss first. Would that be all right? You would not mind, I think. Just one kiss before I eat your sins.

(She gets down on her knees, bends over him, and kisses him long and tenderly on the lips. The Elder Sister watches. The light fades on them and goes out.)

END OF PLAY

Gave Her the Eye

A Paranoid Sexual Fantasy in Ten Minutes

by John Sheehy

CHARACTERS

DONNA
DEX
CLARISSA

Gave Her the Eye

A bar. Donna, still dressed from work, sits alone at one table. Toward the back Clarissa, dressed a little cheaply, sits alone at another table. Dex, also dressed from work, enters with a couple of drinks.

DEX: Here we go.

DONNA: Oh, thank God.

DEX: There. *(She sips.)* Is it all right?

DONNA: Oh, yeah, fine.

DEX: Thanks for coming out with me.

DONNA: Oh, sure.

DEX: You didn't totally want to, hunh?

DONNA: No, hey, I…

DEX: No, that's okay, I mean I appreciate that. It's a good sign.

DONNA: Really? A good sign?

DEX: Yeah. *(Pause.)* Can I ask you a question?

DONNA: Of course.

DEX: I mean, it's kind of personal.

DONNA: Oh…uh…sure.

DEX: It is also…kind of…vitally important.

DONNA: Well, Jesus…

DEX: You swear you'll give me a straight answer?

DONNA: If I can, I guess.

DEX: Listen. *(He checks that no one is listening in.)* You are a human being, aren't you?

DONNA: Yeah…

DEX: No, I mean—You are human?

DONNA: Yes.

DEX: I mean 100 percent.

DONNA: Yes, what do you…?

DEX: I'm sorry but…

DONNA: Look, maybe this wasn't a good idea …

DEX: No, no, I'm sorry. I know this is sounding weird.

DONNA: No, no…it's me. I'm just not used to…being quizzed on, like, my species, you know?

DEX: If you'll let me explain…

DONNA: I don't think…

DEX: Please, let me show you something.

DONNA: I…um…definitely don't want you showing me anything, all right? I think I better go.

DEX: Five minutes. Please. Really, it's important. I don't know how much time I actually have.

DONNA: Hey, I thought you were some kind of normal guy, you know?

DEX: So did I.

DONNA: Well, there you go.

(She starts to exit, he stops her.)

DEX: No…it's just… I thought I was normal, too, a couple days ago. Here just sit down. Give me a couple of minutes and let me show you something. Please, please. I'm not going to hurt you or anything. Please? (She begrudgingly sits back down.) Now, I'm going to show you something but you have to stay calm.

DONNA: Listen, I try not to get involved in situations where people feel it's necessary to tell me to stay calm.

DEX: Five minutes, please.

DONNA: All right.

DEX: (He takes out a pair of sunglasses.) Now, here, anybody looking?

(They both check around. When the coast is clear, he takes out one of his eyeballs and immediately puts on the sunglasses.)

DONNA: What? What are you doing?

DEX: Relax. Here, look at this. (He hands her the eye.)

DONNA: Mother of God!

DEX: Shhhhhhh! Calm down. Don't drop it.

DONNA: I got to go.

DEX: Donna, please. You may be the only person I can trust.

DONNA: What is this?

DEX: My eye.

DONNA: I can see that!

DEX: Keep it down.

DONNA: Easy for you to say.

DEX: Just…look at it. It's not human. Look at it. Careful, don't let anyone see you. Look at the back of it. See those electronic connection things at the back?

DONNA: Jesus!

DEX: One morning, It just popped it out. I was standing at the sink. I felt like hell. There was this big office party. I don't remember half of it. Hung over, or so I thought. I had all this gunk in my eye, and I was washing my face, trying to clean up. I was rubbing my eye right there, you know, in the corner of my eye, and I heard this loud click in my head and my eye just came right out in my hand.

DONNA: I'm going to be sick.

DEX: Yeah, you don't want to see the socket. It's like all covered with these fiber-optic connection points. They did something to me.

DONNA: They?

DEX: Yeah.

DONNA: They who?

DEX: How do I know?

DONNA: What is all this?

DEX: I know this sounds crazy.

DONNA: Sounds crazy? No, more like flat-out crazy.

DEX: They are turning me into a machine, like all the rest.

DONNA: Oh, shut up. Like all the rest…

DEX: No, listen… When I put my eye out, that first time, I was like totally freaking. I mean I was running out the door, half-dressed, when I suddenly remembered this like dream from the night before. I mean, I thought it had to be like some kind of dream, right, but then I started to remember the actual, you know, sensations of coming to in a hospital bed in the middle of some kind of operation on my head.

DONNA: Gross…

DEX: Yeah, and everyone is like shitting that I'm coming to, people are running and yelling at each other, then I guess someone gave me a shot and I was out again. But I remember Kathleen, you know, the branch manager, pitching a fit to kill. I mean she was bitching out this doctor about how "80 percent of the district had been successfully replaced, and if you jeopardize that by screwing up this one simple accountant replacement…"

DONNA: This is way too whacked for me.

DEX: I know, I know. I thought I was going crazy.

DONNA: Hold the thought!

DEX: No! I mean, look me in the eye and tell me this is normal.

DONNA: Which one?

DEX: I need you. You are the only person I can turn to…

DONNA: Me? You are a one-eyed nut!

DEX: Look, people are being replaced. Think about it. Think of the people you know.

DONNA: I hardly know anyone. I just moved here.

DEX: I know, that's why you are probably the only person here I can trust. Think of the people at work. You are like the only person there that makes any mistakes…

DONNA: Hey!

DEX: No, not big ones. Little ones. Little slip-ups, like misplacing messages, forgetting something on your desk and having to go back for it. Little things. But no one else even seems to blink in that place. Look, all I'm saying, I am being changed, and while I am not completely human anymore…I…uh…I do know that there are…parts of me that still work the way they always did, if you know what I mean?

DONNA: I'm gone.

DEX: Listen, I may be the only man that knows that this is going on. Clearly, I was never intended to know as much as I do, but nothing can be done about that now… I just… Look, I'm scared, okay? I am really scared and I figure, you, you, you're too new to have been changed and I… I…just need a little human contact.

DONNA: Not from this human.

DEX: Don't dismiss this. Please, just promise me, think about it. And for your safety and mine, don't mention this to anyone. *(He takes back his eye.)* I better put this back in before it gets too dry. Please think about it. *(He exits.)*

DONNA: Mother of God! *(She downs her drink. She starts to leave but sits back down, starts again but only gets about as far as Clarissa.)*

CLARISSA: *(High-pitched squeaky voice.)* Ah, go ahead.

DONNA: Excuse me?

CLARISSA: Stick around. Wait for him.

DONNA: I don't think I should…

CLARISSA: Oh, come on! It's not the end of the world. You think he's cute? He likes you. Wait for him.

DONNA: If it's not the end of the world, then I'm definitely not waiting for him.

CLARISSA: Sit down, here. Look, may I speak? I saw him give you the eye.

DONNA: I… I… I… I…

CLARISSA: Calm down. Don't get yourself in a spin! It's a trick. It's like a toy or something. His eye? My foot! Can you believe the extent to which some men will go these days to avoid wearing a condom…

DONNA: What? Wearing a…what…?

CLARISSA: Didn't he give you the whole we-must-procreate-and-save-the-world number?

DONNA: Not exactly…

CLARISSA: He does want to sleep with you, doesn't he?

DONNA: Yeah, but it was more of a you-and-me-against-the-alien-robots number…

CLARISSA: Hunh! Changing it up a bit? Not bad. It's still crap, but it's new crap. He's not resting on his laurels… Anyway, there is no conspiracy, no invasion or whatever he told you.

DONNA: I…don't believe this… I semi-believed him.

CLARISSA: Yeah, well, he's cute and seems nice. It's so crazy…who would believe he was making it up. But you know what…leave if you want… but if you stay, I doubt you'll be sorry. I mean he is really good, like top ten good, and I should know, if you know what I mean? So, stick around, have fun, you can be careful, take precautions…

DONNA: This is probably the sickest thing that has ever happened to me!

CLARISSA: You're young, give it time…

DONNA: I am definitely out of here! *(Donna storms out. Clarissa looks around, takes a cellular phone from her purse and dials, waits.)*

CLARISSA: *(Normal voice.)* Yeah, it's me. He just tried it again. We've got to pick him up tonight. I got a couple of shots of the girl… Yeah…no, we can just eliminate her… Yes, tonight, definitely.
(She hangs up. Blackout.)

END OF PLAY

Love Poem #98
by Regina Taylor

CHARACTERS

MARY

WIFE

EMMANUEL

N.B. Mary, the whore, and Mary, the wife, may be played by the same actress: underneath Mary's raincoat is the wife's housedress and apron.

TIME AND PLACE

The tone is Fifties film noir. A Hammett-like murder mystery.

Love Poem #98

EMMANUEL: I met her in an alley strewn with the refuse of the decaying city that I called home for the past thirty years. I had been following a trail of broken promises glittering like gold. Dropping behind me the wadded-up letters from loved ones who write from the shores of faraway continents. I am Hansel alone in the enchanted forest. *(Pause.)* The scent of her mixed with orange rinds, empty beer cans, dead roses, and pee-stained walls.

I met her in an alley behind the Singho Restaurant on Forty-third and Seventh. Across from the twenty-four-hour girly show. Butterscotch skin, a Pepsodent smile and the eyes of a snake charmer.

I met her in an alley.

(Mary, in platform shoes that attack and scrape the floor, crosses upstage. Emmanuel watches her. She pauses but does not look at him. She exits. Lights out. Mary sings a bittersweet Billie Holiday love ballad. Then: Emmanuel's room. We hear a ticking clock and static from the radio.)

EMMANUEL: I wake up in the middle of the night, my body bathed in her voice. Drowning in the sea of possibilities.

(Ticking clock and static.)

EMMANUEL: Four o'clock in the morning. From my window I can see her making her way across the Verrazano Bridge. *(He turns off the radio.)* I will hound her footsteps. Haunt her waking days.

(Lights out. The radio blares a Screaming Jay Hawkins love tune. As Mary crosses and exits, Emmanuel, following, crosses and exits. Mary crosses back and Emmanuel, close behind, crosses. They exit. Light change.)

EMMANUEL: I lost her in Central Park underneath the tunnel between the Delacorte Theater and the Met where I heard the muffled laughter from inside the Egyptian sarcophagus as Hamlet rowed across the lake dredging the waters for Ophelia's remains.

(Mary enters and sits on park bench, her back to the audience. Emmanuel approaches.)

EMMANUEL: My name's Emmanuel.

MARY: What's it to me?

EMMANUEL: You've been haunting my dreams.

MARY: At least someone's getting some sleep. I'm an insomniac—thirteen years.

EMMANUEL: Your voice has washed me clean. Newborn.

MARY: Never wanted any children pulling at me for milk. They grow teeth. They want more. They always want more.

EMMANUEL: *(Takes out a knife and cuts himself across the palm.)* See, for you I bleed.

MARY: *(Laughs.)* Better save some. Someone may be hungry soon. Go on now—I'm no good at chit-chat.

EMMANUEL: What's your name?

MARY: *(Laughs.)* Mary. Mary Magdalene. Now, shove off—you stink.

EMMANUEL: Maybe, but if I used a little Listerine and soap, maybe I could... You might find me bearable enough to...

MARY: To what—to what—?

EMMANUEL: To let me look upon you—

MARY: You want a look? You want a look? I'll give you the sixty-five-cent tour. *(She opens up her raincoat.)* This right here is where my father held me down and burned me with a frying pan when I was four for spilling Kool-Aid on the carpet. This was from three teenage boys who took turns with my virginity when I was nine. This is from my first boyfriend. He was forty-three and I was twelve and pregnant with his child—right across the belly with the heel of his silver-tipped boots. This one here is my personal favorite—from a true admirer—he tried to carve his initials in my chest. And that there is a gunshot wound—close range. And these—let's just say that I've grown accustomed to the teeth of loved ones.

EMMANUEL: She displayed her jewel-encrusted body—

MARY: So what do you have to offer me—my sweet?
(Light change. Mary in spotlight—lip-synching. We hear Mary's voice over the radio, singing a Billie Holiday tune about the sacrifices of love. As Emmanuel cleans and puts together a gun. He loads it.)

EMMANUEL: I'll protect my love.

MARY: *(In spotlight.)* I carry razors behind my eyelids. I can debone a man in fifteen seconds and leave him bleeding in an alleyway—screaming out my name... *(Mary lip-synchs:)*

RADIO: *(Mary's voice.)* ...How can he dream of me when I haven't slept in thirteen years? Tonight I will visit his bed...
(Emmanuel cocks the gun.)

EMMANUEL: For my love...
(Lights out.)

WIFE: I am his wife. My name is Mary. We married when I was nineteen. A week after I graduated high school. He told my father he would protect me. And that was good enough for my dad. Since that day I've never looked at another. I had my first child the next year. And since then, I've borne him seven more. I have stretch marks all over my body. A boy grows inside me now. He sleeps.

He's never been cruel to me. He's never touched me—not mean. He works hard, he comes home, he goes to his room—he sleeps. We have separate bedrooms. He says that I disturb his sleep… I don't complain. I don't mind working. Since they've had cutbacks at his job. I would never complain to him. It's been over a year now since we stopped going out to movies or to dance. Who has time? He's tired—he says. He's tired. I don't complain. I found a job. I'm a waitress—I work double shifts—then come home, cook, clean, hold the children. It's very hard. Sometimes I don't sleep. And hard for him. I would never say… I never said one word. He says it's in my eyes. The words are in my eyes. My eyes cut him to the bone. I've never said…

He was a good father. A good provider. He was never cruel. He cheated on me once. He confessed. Down on his knees. He cried in my lap. What's to be said? I think… He didn't have to tell me. I didn't have to know. He didn't have to say—but he did.

He says I hold things back. Behind the closed lids. I carry razors in my eyes—he says. I wish that… Never mind. More and more—I don't sleep.

(Lights up on Emmanuel.)

EMMANUEL: (Reads from crumpled paper.) "He's tired—he says. He sleeps more and more. He haunts this house." (Emmanuel walks in circles picking up pieces of crumpled paper.) … Can't find my way back…

(Lights up on Mary.)

MARY: (Reading a crumpled paper.) I am his wife. My name is Mary. I wish that… Never mind.

When I was eighteen. After school I would visit his room. He had a nice apartment in midtown, except it had no view—except for the alley. We would lie down on his bed. He would whisper love poems in my ear as I held his organ in my hand. That's all. He didn't touch me. He wanted me to be untouched when we married. I couldn't tell him—I didn't have the heart to tell him. I never told him—He didn't need to know.

(Emmanuel and Mary lock eyes. Emmanuel assembles gun and loads it .)

MARY/WIFE: Tonight I will visit his bed.

END OF PLAY

A Play for
Three Actors, Gender Variable

Arabian Nights
by David Ives

CHARACTERS

INTERPRETER: Wears loose colorful robes and sandals. May be played by a woman wearing a dark beard.

FLORA: Very ordinary.

NORMAN: Utterly normal. Carries a suitcase.

TIME AND PLACE

Flora's shop. The present.

Arabian Nights

*Up right, a freestanding open doorway with a multicolored bead curtain.
Center, a small, plain wooden table with a white cloth. On it: A frame, a
stone, a gold ring, and a figure of a frog.*

*At lights up, Flora is at the table, dusting the objects with a feather duster.
Through the bead curtain comes the Interpreter, leading in Norman, who
carries a suitcase.*

INTERPRETER: Right this way, sir, this way. The most beautiful shop in the
world. All the wonders of the kingdom. For nothing! Nothing! I will
interpret for you.

NORMAN: *(To Flora.)* Hello.

INTERPRETER: Hail, fair maid! says he.

FLORA: *(To Norman, putting the feather duster away.)* Good morning.

INTERPRETER: All praise to the highest, says she.

NORMAN: Do you…speak any English?

INTERPRETER: Do you…speak any English?

FLORA: *(She speaks perfect, unaccented English.)* Yes, I speak some English.

INTERPRETER: Indeed, sir, I can stammer out a broken song of pitiful, insuffi-
cient words.

NORMAN: Ah-ha.

INTERPRETER: Ah-ha.

NORMAN: Well…

INTERPRETER: A deep hole in the ground.

NORMAN: I…

INTERPRETER: *(Points to his eye.)* The organ of vision.

NORMAN: Ummm…

INTERPRETER: Ummm…

NORMAN: Listen.

INTERPRETER: Do you hear something?
(Interpreter and Flora listen for something.)

NORMAN: I'm sorry to rush in so late like this.

FLORA: No, please.

INTERPRETER: No, please.

NORMAN: But you see…

INTERPRETER: *(Points to his butt.)* But— *(Points to Flora.)* —you— *(Does binoculars with his hands.)* —see…

NORMAN: *(Looks at his watch.)* Darn …

INTERPRETER: *(Produces an hourglass from among his robes.)* How swiftly flow the sands of time!

NORMAN: I know this sounds crazy—

INTERPRETER: I know this sounds crazy—

NORMAN: I only have about ten minutes.

INTERPRETER: Soon the golden orb of heaven will cleave the house of the hedgehog.

NORMAN: I have to catch a plane.

INTERPRETER: I must clamber upon the flying corporate carpet and flap away from your kingdom.

NORMAN: Anyway, I want to find…

INTERPRETER: Anyway, I want to find…

FLORA: Yes?

INTERPRETER: Yes?

NORMAN: I guess you'd call it…

INTERPRETER: Something unparalleled! Something sublime!

NORMAN: A souvenir.

INTERPRETER: *(You're kidding.)* A *souvenir*…?!

NORMAN: Something to take with me.

INTERPRETER: A treasure!

FLORA: Any particular kind of thing?

INTERPRETER: Can the funicular hide the spring?

NORMAN: Excuse me?

INTERPRETER: Accuse me?

FLORA: How much did you want to spend?

INTERPRETER: How much did you want to spend?

NORMAN: It doesn't matter.

INTERPRETER: Let's haggle. I'm loaded!

FLORA: Is this for yourself?

INTERPRETER: Have you a mistress, a wife, a *hareem*?

NORMAN: No, this is for me.

INTERPRETER: Alas, a lad alone in all the world am I.

FLORA: Well…

INTERPRETER: A deep hole in the ground.

FLORA: I think I can help you.

INTERPRETER: Solitary sir, the maiden says, I look in your eyes and I see your soul shining there like a golden carp in an azure pool.

NORMAN: Really…?

INTERPRETER: Really. Now, in this brief moment, in the midst of this mirage called life, here on this tiny square of soil on the whirling earth, I feel the two of us joined by a crystal thread, your soul to my soul to yours.

NORMAN: You do?

INTERPRETER: You do?

FLORA: I do.

INTERPRETER: She does.

NORMAN: You know, I've been up and down this street every day…

INTERPRETER: Day and night I have walked the bazaar…

NORMAN: I sure wish I'd seen this place sooner.

INTERPRETER: Only so that I might see *you.*

FLORA: I've noticed you walking by.

INTERPRETER: How I pined for you to enter as you passed.

NORMAN: You did?

INTERPRETER: She did. She asks your name.

NORMAN: My name is Norman.

INTERPRETER: My name is Sinbad!

NORMAN: I'm here on some business.

INTERPRETER: I am the merchant son of a great prince, exiled from my land.

FLORA: Is that so.

INTERPRETER: Her name is Izthatso.

FLORA: People call me Flora.

INTERPRETER: But people call me Flora.

FLORA: With an F.

INTERPRETER: With an F.

NORMAN: I…

INTERPRETER: The organ of vision.

NORMAN: *(Looks at watch.) Darn* it.

INTERPRETER: *(Produces hourglass.) Darn* it…

NORMAN: Y'know, Flora…

INTERPRETER: Y'know, Flora…

NORMAN: You shop and you shop …

INTERPRETER: We live our brief lives…

NORMAN: …you never seem to find that special thing you're shopping for.

INTERPRETER: …each day awaiting the dawn that will give us purpose, bring us happiness.

FLORA: That's so true.

INTERPRETER: That's so true.

NORMAN: Maybe what I'm looking for is right here.

INTERPRETER: Perhaps my dawn has come.

FLORA: Shhh!

INTERPRETER: Shhh!

FLORA: I thought I heard my father.

INTERPRETER: My father may be listening!

FLORA: It's almost time for his tea.

INTERPRETER: If he sees me talking to you, he'll cut your throat!

NORMAN AND INTERPRETER: *(Simultaneous—as they pick up the suitcase together.)* Maybe I should be going…

FLORA: No—

INTERPRETER: No—

FLORA: He won't bother us.

INTERPRETER: Have mercy, good sir!

NORMAN: *(Hefts suitcase.)* I do have a plane to catch.

INTERPRETER: Take my suitcase.

(Flora takes the suitcase from him and sets it down.)

FLORA: There's plenty of time.

INTERPRETER: Keep your voice low.

FLORA: Shhh!

INTERPRETER: Shhh!

FLORA: I thought I heard him calling.

INTERPRETER: He's sharpening the blade.

(We hear the sound of a blade being sharpened.)

NORMAN: *(Cry of surprise.)*

INTERPRETER: *(Cry of surprise.)*

FLORA: He's watching old movies.

INTERPRETER: The old man is *mad.*

FLORA: Anyway, I'm sure I'll have something you'll like.

INTERPRETER: Act as if you're buying something.

NORMAN: What about these things right here?

INTERPRETER: What about these things right here?

FLORA: Maybe a picture frame?

INTERPRETER: Can you conceive, prince, how lonely my life is? It is as empty as this frame.

FLORA: Or a stone?

INTERPRETER: It is as hard—and as cheap—as this stone.

FLORA: *(Gestures left.)* I have more in the back.

INTERPRETER: *(Gestures left.)* He keeps me locked in a tiny cell.

NORMAN: No. No.

INTERPRETER: Stay with me.

FLORA: Maybe…

INTERPRETER: What I long for…

FLORA: …a golden ring?

INTERPRETER: …is love. Golden love.

FLORA: If not a ring, maybe a figurine?

INTERPRETER: But my father has betrothed me to a man as ugly as this frog.

FLORA: Interested?

INTERPRETER: Would *you* marry this?

NORMAN: Not really.

INTERPRETER: Not really.

FLORA: I don't know what else I can show you.

INTERPRETER: I have nothing, sir. Nothing! Nichts! Neets! Niente! Rien! Zip zero nada zilch! Bupkis!

NORMAN: My God, you're beautiful.

INTERPRETER: My God, you're beautiful.

FLORA: Excuse me?

INTERPRETER: Excuse me?

NORMAN: I'm sorry.

INTERPRETER: I'm sorry.

NORMAN: I don't usually say things like that.

INTERPRETER: I know I sound like a jerk.

NORMAN: Sometimes it's something so simple.

INTERPRETER: So complicated are the ways of kismet.

NORMAN: You walk into a shop…

INTERPRETER: I look at you…

NORMAN: …and everything's suddenly different, somehow.

INTERPRETER: …and my heart flutters inside me like a leaf of the perfumed gum tree at the scented bounce of bedspring.

FLORA: Really?

INTERPRETER: Really.

NORMAN: Now in this brief moment…

INTERPRETER: Now in this brief moment…

NORMAN: On this tiny patch of ground on the whirling earth…

INTERPRETER: In the midst of this mirage called life…

NORMAN: I feel us joined by a crystal thread, your soul to my soul to yours.

INTERPRETER: Etcetera, etcetera, etcetera.

FLORA: You do?

INTERPRETER: You do?

NORMAN: I…

INTERPRETER: The organ of vision.

NORMAN: …do.

INTERPRETER: He does.

NORMAN: How can I leave, now that I've seen you, met you, heard you?

INTERPRETER: How can I get on a plane?

NORMAN: Now that fate has brought me to this bazaar?

INTERPRETER: It's so bizarre. But fate has decreed that we must part.

NORMAN: *(Takes out an hourglass.)* O cruel fate! How swiftly flow the sands of time!

INTERPRETER: *(Looks at a watch.)* Shit… !

NORMAN: The stars have decreed we must part.

INTERPRETER: Look, I really gotta go.

NORMAN: *(Kisses Flora's hand.)* But I will return, O my florid queen!

INTERPRETER: Maybe I'll pass this way again sometime.

FLORA: I will wait for you, my Norman prince!

NORMAN: Izthatso.

FLORA: It *is* so! I will be yours and you will be mine and we will be…

INTERPRETER: …each other's.

NORMAN: …each other's.

FLORA: …each other's.

INTERPRETER: Maybe I'll have something you like.

NORMAN: Well…

INTERPRETER: A deep hole in the ground.

FLORA: Well…

INTERPRETER: With purest water at the bottom.

NORMAN: Salaam!

INTERPRETER: So long!

FLORA: Salaam!

INTERPRETER: So long! So long! So long!

NORMAN: Open, sesame!

> (Norman whirls out, followed by the Interpreter.)

FLORA: (Sighs.) Oh, well. (She takes out the feather duster—and it's been changed into a large red rose.) Shazam!

> (She starts to dust the objects with it. Blackout.)

END OF PLAY